OL

Olivier Rolin was ⎯⎯⎯⎯⎯⎯⎯ ⎯⎯ is a critically acclaimed author and freelance writer. His books have won many prizes, including the Prix du Style for *Stalin's Meteorologist* in 2014. He first visited Russia, then the USSR, in 1986. Since then, he has returned many times and has travelled widely throughout the country.

Over the last thirty-six years **Ros Schwartz** has translated some seventy-five works of fiction and non-fiction. Her new translation of Saint-Exupéry's *The Little Prince* was published in 2010, and she is currently involved in Penguin Classics' project to retranslate George Simenon's oeuvre. In 2009 she was made a Chevalier de l'Ordre des Arts et des Lettres.

ALSO BY OLIVIER ROLIN IN ENGLISH
TRANSLATION

Hotel Crystal
Paper Tiger

OLIVIER ROLIN

Stalin's Meteorologist

One man's untold story of love,
life and death

TRANSLATED FROM THE FRENCH BY
Ros Schwartz

VINTAGE

1 3 5 7 9 10 8 6 4 2

Vintage
20 Vauxhall Bridge Road,
London SW1V 2SA

Vintage is part of the Penguin Random House group of companies
whose addresses can be found at global.penguinrandomhouse.com

Copyright © Éditions du Seuil/Éditions Paulsen 2014
Plate section images copyright © Mémorial/Éditions Paulsen
English translation copyright © Ros Schwartz 2017

Olivier Rolin has asserted his right to be identified as the author of this
Work in accordance with the Copyright, Designs and Patents Act 1988

First published in Vintage in 2018
First published in hardback by Harvill Secker in 2017
First published with the title *Le météorologue* in France by
Éditions du Seuil in 2014

penguin.co.uk/vintage

A CIP catalogue record for this book is available from the British Library

ISBN 9781784701758

This book has been selected to receive financial assistance from
English PEN's "PEN Translates!" programme, supported by Arts
Council England. English PEN exists to promote literature and our
understanding of it, to uphold writers' freedoms around the world,
to campaign against the persecution and imprisonment of writers
for stating their views, and to promote the friendly co-operation of
writers and the free exchange of ideas. www.englishpen.org

This book is supported by the Institut français (Royaume-Uni)
as part of the Burgess programme

Printed and bound in Great Britain by Clays Ltd, Elcograf S.p.A.

Penguin Random House is committed to a sustainable future
for our business, our readers and our planet. This book is made
from Forest Stewardship Council® certified paper.

For Masha

And I thought and I read
According to the Bible of the breezes

Sergey Yesenin,
'Soil, Soil Soil' in *The Collected Poems*

I

I

He was an expert on clouds. The long cirrus ice quills, the swollen, towering cumulonimbi, the torn ragged strati, the stratocumuli that ruffle the sky like wavelets left in the sand by the receding tide, the altostrati that veil the sun, and all the vast, drifting shapes rimmed with light, the fluffy giants that produce rain and snow and lightning. But he didn't have his head in the clouds – or at least I don't think he did. From what I know of him, there is nothing to suggest he was an eccentric. He represented the USSR at the International Commission on Clouds, he spoke at pan-Soviet congresses on the formation of fog, and in 1930 he set up the Weather Bureau. But these lyrical names didn't set him dreaming. As a scientist doing his job in the interests – of course – of building socialism he took it all seriously; he was no comic-strip Professor Nimbus.

Clouds were not his excuse to dream, there was nothing nebulous about him; I suspect him even of a certain starchiness. Appointed the first director of the USSR's

Hydrometeorological Centre in 1929, he set out to establish a water registry as well as a wind and a sunshine registry. He probably saw nothing romantic in that, no invitation to reverie in mapping the intangible. It was the concrete that interested him, measurable realities, the collision of huge masses of air, the low-water levels of rivers, ice-dammed rivers and meltdowns, rainfall, and the effect of these phenomena on farming and on the lives of Soviet citizens. Socialism was being built in the sky too.

He was born in 1881 in Krapivno, a village in Ukraine . . .

Before chronicling the life and death of this man dedicated to the peaceful observation of nature who was crushed by the fury of history, I shall say a few words about the circumstances that led me to cross his path, long after his disappearance (here the word takes on its full significance, as we shall see). Stories don't appear out of the blue or from the clouds, so it seems a good idea for them to present their credentials. In 2010, I'd been invited to speak at the University of Arkhangelsk. I was greeted with the warmth that is typical of Russian life, alongside a great deal of indifference and even roughness. A Welcome banner was unfurled and people brought out photos from an earlier trip (I'm a regular visitor there). The only downside was that the photos showed how much time had gone by, but it was touching all the same. I was treated perhaps not like a president, but let's say a sub-prefect. I love Arkhangelsk because its name means Archangel, because of the wide estuary on which it stands and which, in winter, you traverse on planks laid on the ice festooned at night with pale lights, because of the wooden houses that were still quite common when I first used to visit (few, since, have withstood the property developers), and because it seems to me that girls are particularly beautiful here (I remember girls gliding on roller skates on the embankment along the Dvina one May, their bare, tanned legs, hair flying in the wind, escorted by dragonflies – my equivalent of Proust's girls on bicycles. I vaguely recall that Blaise Cendrars talks somewhere of the golden bells (or golden belfries?) of Arkhangelsk, but I can't find it anywhere. It doesn't matter: writers are not only what they have written, but what we think they have written.

Then I took the small plane (an Antonov An-24, to be precise), which twice a week flies between Arkhangelsk and the Solovetsky Islands, an archipelago in the White Sea. When the sea is frozen, as it is six months of the year, there is no other way of getting there. The man sitting next to me on the plane was a young Orthodox priest with a mop of frizzy hair who looked like Georges Perec (I'm not sure whether Perec would have welcomed the comparison, or the priest, had he known who Perec was, but I found that there was a strong resemblance). The holy man was holding an e-reader which I then thought to be the pinnacle of a modernity that I had not yet attained, and which seemed incongruous in a priest, especially Russian Orthodox. The hi-tech object had a leather cover decorated with an icon of the Virgin Mary on which he bestowed profuse kisses.

I covertly peeked at his screen, hoping that it was an erotic novel, but I have to admit that it wasn't.

It was the beauty of the place, seen in photographs, that had prompted me to undertake this journey. And I'd barely stepped out of the little air terminal built of blue-painted planks when the sight of the high walls, the squat towers and (golden . . .) belfries of the monastery-stronghold stretching along an isthmus between a bay and a lake shrouded in snow convinced me I'd been right to come here. The same beauty as Mont Saint-Michel except that it was completely the opposite: a monastic and military monument, and a prison, in the middle of the sea, which extends horizontally, whereas Mont Saint-Michel soars vertically. Here, no crowds, no tourist tat. I hiked around the island, a black-and-white landscape of frozen lakes and coniferous forests that glowed blood red at sunset. I found sanctuary in a tiny hotel called Priyut – the shelter. Katia, the owner, was charming, extremely cheerful (admittedly, despite my Russophilia which friends tease me about, this is quite unusual), pretty (perhaps the rather outmoded adjective 'buxom' would be more apt), and her kindness stretched to telling me that I spoke her language very well. From my room in the evening I could see the walls and the scaly onion domes blazing across the ice. I had no idea that the first seeds of a book were being planted inside me – but that's always the way, it creeps up on you.

The monastery, founded in the fifteenth century by hermit monks, is one of the oldest in Russia. Each era has left its stamp, and from 1923, the monastery housed (if that is the word) the first camp of what was to become the Main Directorate for Camps and Detention Facilities, the *Glavnoye upravlenie ispravitelno-trudovykh lagerey*, sadly known by its notorious acronym, the Gulag. On my return, I set about reading all the books I could find on its history. That was how I learned that in the camp there had been a library of 30,000 volumes, made up directly or indirectly of books belonging to the deportees, many of whom were nobles or intellectuals (*byvshy intelligentny chelovek* or *bich* 'ex-intellectual' in the language of the secret police). Gradually the idea of making a film was born, and in April 2012 I returned to the Solovetsky Islands to scout locations.

I was welcomed by Antonina Sochina, one of the island's human memories. She was a delightful, lively, elderly lady, with reddish blonde hair and blue eyes, dressed in jeans and a roll-neck sweater. Her house was full of books and plants, she made wonderful jams with the berries that all Russians love – bilberries, cranberries and another, whose name I don't know, a sort of orange-coloured raspberry called *moroshka* which grows in marshy areas and is so delicious that Pushkin is said to have asked for some on his deathbed (berries and mushrooms are a staple of the Russian diet and of its folklore; curiously the generic word for berries, *yagoda*, was also the surname of the head of the intelligence service and secret police, the *Gosudarstvennoye politicheskoye upravlenie* (GPU), later the NKVD, from 1934 to 1936: Genrikh Yagoda, who is to play a role in the next part of this story). Among the books that Antonina showed me there was one that had a cover with a picture of clouds, an album not for general sale, published by the daughter of a deportee in memory of her father. Alexey Feodosievich Wangenheim, the meteorologist, had been deported to the Solovetsky Islands in 1934. Half of the book comprised reproductions of letters he had sent from the camp to his daughter, Eleonora, who was not yet four at the time of his arrest. There were pressed flowers and coloured illustrations of plants, drawn with a confident hand in crayon or watercolour, simple and clear. There were pictures of the aurora borealis, frozen seas, an Arctic fox, a hen, a watermelon, a samovar, an aeroplane, boats, a cat, a fly, a candle and birds. The dried flowers and the drawings were beautiful, but they had not been composed solely to be visually pleasing: they had an educational purpose. The father was using plants to teach his daughter the basics of arithmetic and geometry. The lobes of a leaf represented the elementary numbers, its shape symmetry and asymmetry, while a pine cone illustrated the spiral. The drawings were answers to riddles.

I was moved by this long-distance conversation between a father and his very young daughter, whom he would never see again, his determination to play a part in her education despite being far away. And I was moved by the daughter's steadfast love for the father she had known so fleetingly, to which the commemorative book I leafed through at Antonina's bore witness. He was, Eleonora said, an accomplished pianist, and she remembered hearing him play the 'Appassionata,' the 'Moonlight' Sonata and Schubert's Impromptus. He was fond of Pushkin and Lermontov. Until 1956, the year of his posthumous rehabilitation, she wrote, my mother waited for him to come back. When I misbehaved, she added, my mother would tell me that I'd be ashamed when my father came home. Judging myself through his eyes became the rule by which I lived. The idea of writing the story of this man, one of the millions of victims of Stalin's madness, began to stir in me. Later, in Moscow, meeting people who had known Eleonora at the end of her life did the rest. She became a renowned palaeontologist. I never had the opportunity to meet her: she had died not long before, in circumstances I shall describe. I regret that she didn't live long enough to know that the album she dedicated to her father's memory had the unforeseeable consequence of sparking another book, far away, in another country, in another language.

3

He was born in 1881, in Krapivno, a village in Ukraine whose name means 'the place where nettles grow'. There are a lot of nettles in South Russia and in Ukraine and consequently there are a lot of Krapivnos (the name appears in the third line of Isaac Babel's *Red Cavalry*). His village was on the outskirts of the little town of Nizhyn, whose high school has the honour of counting Gogol as an alumnus. His father, Feodosy Petrovich Wangenheim, was a *barin*, a minor nobleman, a deputy at the *zemstvo*, the regional council set up by Alexander II. The family's very un-Russian name suggests a distant Dutch origin, possibly a ship's carpenter who came to build Peter the Great's fleet and was rewarded by being given a piece of land in Ukraine. A photograph shows Feodosy Petrovich as a man with a pleasant face framed by waves of grey hair and a bushy beard, and perhaps a slightly lecherous look. I imagine him like a character out of Chekhov – idealistic, loquacious, full of woolly ideas about social progress, a womaniser, a gambler, weak. He prided himself on his knowledge of agronomy and he planted an experimental field in the village of Uyutnoye, which lay on the railway line from Moscow and Kiev to Voronezh. On summer evenings in Uyutnoye, after inspecting his blackcurrants, gooseberry bushes and raspberry canes and watching the sun turn red beyond the rye fields, he would sit beneath the veranda in the company of women in light, swishing dresses, chatting with the doctor and the investigating magistrate over a cigar and brandy, discussing the education of the masses and criticising the Tsar's authoritarianism. One of the girls, sitting at the piano, plays a little piece by Schubert, or maybe Chopin. Pure conjecture. Daughters, on the other hand, it is a known fact that he had four with his wife Maria Kuvshinnikova, and three boys, including Alexey, the cloud enthusiast. In any case, it was certain he was not reactionary because after the Revolution he refused to emigrate like one of his sons, Nikolay, and became an advisor to the People's Commissariat of Land Cultivation. And he allowed all his children – even the girls! – to study the sciences.

I'd like to think that watching the clouds rolling above the infinite plain sparked off Alexey Feodosievich's curiosity about meteors. Painters and writers have depicted this Russian or Ukrainian rural landscape countless times. A dizzying profundity of space, a vastness where everything seems immobile, a silence broken only by the cries of birds – quails, cuckoos, hoopoes, crows. Wheat or barley fields, expanses of blue grass dotted with yellow wormwood flowers, bounded by a rutted path. Birch and slender poplar groves, the golden domes of a church gleam in the distance, the roofs of a village, the occasional thin glint of a river: it is the landscape of *The Steppe* (which is set in this borderland between Ukraine and Russia), 'At Home' and many other short stories by Chekhov, who was writing during those years. It is the landscape of Yesenin's poetry, of Ivan Shishkin's and Isaac Levitan's paintings. Sometimes, far off in the immense distance, the funnel of a steam engine is a reminder that in the heart of this apparently frozen time something new is happening, which could possibly be progress but might also be a threat. And, overhead, in a sky exalted by the vast flatness of the land, the clouds 'irregular and marvellously rotund' which the young narrator contemplates dreamily in *The Life of Arsenyev* by Ivan Bunin, the menacing clouds which the landscape artist Savrasov painted in 1881, the year Alexey Feodosievich was born, cast giant shadows over the shimmering fields.

Those landscapes devoured by emptiness can also be seen in some colour photographs taken at the beginning of the twentieth century by another noble passionate about science and technology, Sergey Prokudin-Gorsky, who scoured the Empire, from the forests of Karelia to central Asia, to build up a photographic archive – 3,500 plates, just under 2,000 of which have been preserved. This photographer-inventor, whose self-portrait beside a river in Georgia shows a long, mournful, bespectacled face with a drooping moustache beneath a soft hat, bears witness, like Chekhov, like his friend Isaac Levitan, like Bunin, like – in their own way – the Wangenheims father and son, to an era when Russian history seemed to be taking a different, more peaceful, more enlightened course, than the dark, terrible one to come. The striking thing about his plates is not just the miraculous fidelity of the colours, but the way they give the viewer the feeling of being literally sucked towards the line where the sky and earth meet. What lies beyond, over there? Nothing. The edge of the world, perhaps, or the infinite repetition of the same things. Woods, fields, the steppe, paths, crows' flights, tiny bell-towers beneath the clouds. Russia is a forest, *les*, and Russia is a plain, *pole*. And Russia is space, *prostor*. I do not know much for certain or of significance about my character's childhood, but I am certain that space played a part in his formative years.

And so I would like to imagine that lying in the grass like Bunin's Arsenyev, Alexey Feodosievich dreamed one day: 'What breathtaking beauty! I wish I could climb on to that cloud and float away, drift among those terrifying heights, in the immensity of the sky . . .' Maybe he did dream of doing so. But I think the truth is probably simpler and more prosaic: it was his father who passed on his vocation. Because the decidedly curious Feodosy Petrovich also dabbled in meteorology, having built a small weather station on his land. It was at home that Alexey first learned about the land and the sky, attending regional agricultural conferences with his father, studying the magnetic anomaly of the

Kursk region, proposing a new method for calculating the number of plants per square metre (more reminiscent of Flaubert's *Bouvard and Pécuchet* than Chekhov), and, in Uyutnoye, reading the graphs traced by the little styluses of the recording instruments on rolls of graph paper – rainfall, humidity, atmospheric pressure, the strength and direction of the wind. He graduated from the Orel gymnasium with very good or excellent marks in all subjects: Greek, Latin, maths, catechism, French – curiously it was only in geography that his marks were merely 'satisfactory'. At the turn of the century he gained admission to the mathematics department of Moscow University's faculty of physics and mathematics, and got himself expelled almost immediately for taking part in the student protests of 1901. In Russia, they don't do things by halves, especially protests, and the minister of public education was assassinated by a Socialist Revolutionary student.

Alexey certainly didn't go to such extremes. In reply to the dean who questioned him he stated that in principle he was against violence, but admitted that he had attended meetings and voted, and he was thrown out.

Next came military service, followed by the Kiev Polytechnic Institute where he earned a diploma (with distinction) in the speed of cyclones. He then enrolled at the Moscow Agricultural Institute, but had not yet chosen between the earth and the sky; he wrote articles comparing the respective merits of natural fertilisers and minerals in the smoking process – again more akin to *Bouvard and Pécuchet* – then he taught mathematics at the girls' gymnasium in Dmitriev, a small town north of Kursk. Let us move on quickly, we're not writing his CV, but all the same, in Dmitriev he did something important: in 1906 he married the history and geography teacher Yuliya Bolotova. They had a daughter together who would become a renowned psychiatrist. His next step was the Caspian hydro-meteorological department, in Petrovsk (modern-day Makhachkala) where he researched variations in the level of this landlocked sea – a problem that had fascinated Alexandre Dumas during his voyage to the Caucasus and which led him to come up with the hare-brained hypothesis of a sort of valve that would open and shut natural channels between the Caspian Sea and the Persian Gulf. Then came war and Alexey was called up to head the weather forecasting service of the 8th Army, fighting the Austrians in Galicia. Forecasting which direction the wind would come from and whether rain was on the way was important for gas attacks, and that was how war was waged at the time, both in the East and in the West. Then it was the Revolution, and he was back in Dmitriev. The fronts of civil war shifted; unlike his brother Nikolay he was not on the side of the Whites, who took the town. He hid on a farm; the Reds recaptured it and he was made inspector for the People's Commissariat for Education. He organised agitprop meetings in the villages, sported a Lenin-style goatee beard and wore boots, a dark peajacket and a cap. Head agronomist of the oblast, he set up little weather stations in various places whose data would help improve the harvests, but he often had difficulty convincing the *muzhiks* (peasants) that weather vanes, anemometers and other whirligigs and little dishes were not evil devices to blame for the droughts.

4

Ten years passed, and now we are at the beginning of the 1930s. He has divorced his first wife and married Varvara Kurguzova whom he met in Dmitriev where she was director of School Number 40. He was living in Petrograd, where he was in charge of long-range weather forecasting for the main Geophysical Observatory, but now he lives in Moscow, where he has just been appointed head of the USSR's newly established unified Hydrometeorological Service. He is a Party member. A bourgeois Communist, he sits on countless committees and sub-committees, presidiums and scientific advisory boards. He knows Maxim Gorky and Nadezhda Krupskaya, Lenin's widow, Anatoly Lunacharsky, the Soviet People's Commissar of Education, and the great scientist and Arctic explorer Otto Yulyevich Schmidt, who is only at the start of his illustrious career. In the *Great Soviet Encyclopaedia*, Wangenheim is listed alongside Van Gogh. It looks as if he is well on the way to becoming a member of the Academy of Sciences and being decorated with the Order of Lenin, etc. In a contemporary photo, his face looks much fuller than in his Dmitriev days. He has shaved off his goatee, keeping only a pencil moustache, and he has his father's wavy hair. He is wearing a white shirt beneath a dark jacket, and a knitted tie with a tiepin. He really looks like a big shot, but did Lenin himself ever look unkempt? With Vladimir Ilich too, it was always tie and pin, waistcoat and watch chain. In this garb, in a three-piece suit of bronze or stone, Lenin has continued to rouse phantom crowds in every square in Russia, up until today.

Establishing a unified hydrology and meteorology service over the entire territory of the USSR is no small matter; that territory, as was trumpeted in Soviet propaganda – and for once it was true – covering 'a sixth of the Earth's land surface'. A vast continent – wild, semi-desert, almost without roads, bounded in the north by the Arctic Ocean, running from Poland to Alaska, and bordering Japan, China, Mongolia, Afghanistan, Iran and Turkey, furrowed by the Pamir, Altai and Caucasus mountains, scorching hot in the steppes of central Asia, covered in snow and ice for a good part of the year, striated with great rivers, from the Volga to the Amur . . . Twenty-two and a half million square kilometres . . . Eleven time zones in those days (now there are only nine). Russia is 'that land that does not care to do things by halves, but has spread a vast plain over half the world', wrote Nikolay Gogol (exaggerating somewhat) of Wangenheim's country. This is a different scale altogether, compared with Uyutnoye or even the Dmitriev region . . . Today, as I write, it is –39 degrees centigrade in Yakutsk, +17 degrees centigrade in Sochi, while a deep depression of 968 millibars is approaching the Kamchatka peninsula. Thousands of kilometres from there another is developing in the Barents Sea to the west of the Novaya Zemlya archipelago, whereas there is high pressure of 1034 millibars over the centre of Siberia. Building a system capable of taking the temperature of this colossus each day and producing forecasts is a crushing task, especially since it involves overcoming the resistance of tangled bureaucracies each jealous of its territory, and we know that administrative inertia is one of the legacies from the Tsarist era which the Soviet regime managed splendidly to turn to advantage.

Alexey Feodosievich sets to work with energy, and even passion. Curiously, later, in his letters, he often refers to the unified Hydrometeorological Service as 'my dear/beloved Soviet child'. He battles officialdom, forces the hand of the republics and shakes up the *narkoms* – the various People's Commissars – making them all delegate the sections of sky and water which they believe belong to them. He extends his network of forecasting stations, he receives news of the winds in Sakhalin, the thousands of cubic metres of water per second flowing down the Yenisey river, the ice blocking the Northern Sea Route, which we in western Europe call the Northeast Passage, and the millimetres of rain that have or have not fallen on the Ukraine plains. Just as Genrikh Yagoda, head of the GPU, is supposed to know everything about Soviet citizens' declared opinions and even more their secret thoughts, so he, Alexey Feodosievich Wangenheim, is the spymaster who probes, collects and records the continent's moods. Aircraft need his intelligence to land, ships to navigate a passage across the Kara Sea, tractors to plough their furrows in the *chernozem* (black earth). On 1 January 1930 the first weather forecast is broadcast on the radio, on 3350 metres long wave. Naturally these forecasts aren't for the benefit of holidaymakers or weekenders, who are few at the time in the land of the international proletariat, but for the construction of socialism, and more specifically of socialist agriculture.

And, God knows, socialist agriculture needs help. Stalin's insane policy combining the elimination of rich or supposedly affluent peasant farmers (sometimes owning one cow was enough to be decreed a kulak and to be deported or shot), with forced collectivisation and the requisitioning of grain, results in a terrible famine in Ukraine. Some three million people will die between 1932 and 1933 in the region where Alexey Feodosievich spent his childhood and youth. When people have eaten all the cats, dogs and insects, gnawed the bones of dead animals, chewed grasses, roots and leather, they sometimes eat the dead, and on occasion even help them to die. In *Everything Flows*, Vasily Grossman describes these terrible times when entire villages, silent and pestilential, house nothing but dead bodies, where, every morning, carts collect the corpses of children come to beg in the streets of Kiev. Then, of course, it is not weather forecasts that the rural areas need, but simply a little humanity. But does *he* know that? Does he know it more than the others, the millions of others who are unaware, or who choose to be unaware, that the famous 'construction of socialism' leaves so much suffering in its wake, who continue to believe that in the Soviet Union a new humanity is being born, freed from its chains? Who ignore or accept the famine (believing it is the price to be paid, and after all the victims are backward, reactionary peasants), as they will ignore or accept the mass deportations and deaths in the Gulag? Stalin knows of course that the Ukraine countryside is dying, yet persists with his fatal policy because it cannot be said that he is wrong, and also to crush a peasantry he considers to be a class enemy; the high-ranking officials in the Kremlin know, the Kaganoviches, the Voroshilovs, the Molotovs, who are no more than senior lackeys, but even supposing they do not share Stalin's views, they would never dare oppose him. But Alexey Feodosievich is not a high-ranking official. The hydro-meteorological department isn't the People's Commissariat of Internal Affairs, he probably doesn't know that the cobs being harvested in the fields of his youth are human heads. He believes that the rumours he has heard – if he did hear any – the quickly hushed-up rumours, because people repeating them risk their lives, are slander cooked up by the inexhaustibly destructive imagination of the enemies of the Revolution. The formidable killing machine is also a machine for obliterating death, which makes it all the more formidable. He continues to perfect his network of weather stations, refine his forecasts and broadcast his bulletins on long wave, quietly certain that he is helping with the construction of socialism and in particular improving the farming yield.

And he takes a broad and ambitious view. In his field, he is a visionary, or perhaps a utopian. Not content with casting his net over the vast territory of the Soviet Union, he dreams of a global meteorological system. Of course, he believes that to achieve this, the proletarian revolution will have to triumph throughout the entire world, and he is in no doubt that this will eventually come to pass. Political conjecture is risky, but scientific forecasting, bold as it is, has proved accurate. In two or three clicks, on my screen I can see a depression approaching the Kamchatka peninsula, another heading for Novaya Zemlya, gales blowing over the Okhotsk Sea, curves showing high pressure areas in wide bands over the centre of Siberia, I learn that it is −31 in Kolomenskoye, on the infamous Kolyma river, −5 in Arkhangelsk, +5 in Astrakhan, and zero in Kiev where the people have just overthrown a dictator; and if I'm interested in South America, far away in the other hemisphere, it's 28 degrees in Santiago de Chile where the sun's shining, as it is in Buenos Aires where it's only 22 degrees, while gentle high-pressure curves snake from Juan Fernández island, where the real Robinson Crusoe lived, to the Pampas, straddling the Andes cordillera on their way: Wangenheim's dream has come about, without waiting for an increasingly unlikely world proletarian revolution. Electronic bugs with golden forewings and blue silica wings, dozens of satellites rotate in the dark sky, monitoring the clouds, the rain, the ocean currents, the temperatures, sea levels, the melting of the ice: this is the world revolution (nowadays called 'globalisation').

And then, in the domain of what we now call 'energy transition', Alexey Feodosievich really is a prophet. If he has established a 'wind registry', it is because he has the vision of a forest of wind turbines stretching from the Bering Strait and the Kamchatka peninsula to the shores of the Black Sea, supplying energy to the frozen wastes of the north and the scorching deserts of the south – and, as is common knowledge, 'Communism is Soviet power plus electrification of the whole country.' 'Not only does our country have immense wind power,' he writes, in 1935, 'it is renewable and inexhaustible. It will enable us to combat drought and tame deserts, wherever we find strong, scorching winds, and wherever it is very difficult to transport fuel to. The wind can transform deserts into oases. In the north, the wind will provide heat and light.' He will write this in a letter to his wife, from the Solovetsky Islands where he was deported, and where for six months of the year, the wind makes the huge trees creak and sway and freezes the backs of the *zeks* (convicts) marching in columns along the snow-covered path. While there, he reads a brief article about wind power in a magazine, and ruminates bitterly that he had been a pioneer, when he was free: 'All these thoughts were going round in my head and I said to myself that I was the first to tackle these questions with the wind registry project. Soon the vast territories of the USSR will be electrified thanks to wind power, and my name will vanish without trace.' Similarly he launched the 'sun registry' because, even though no device capable of transforming its light existed yet, he foresaw that 'the future belongs to solar energy and wind power'.

Attempts to open the Northeast Passage to shipping are no modern endeavour either. In 1932, well before global warming and the melting of the Arctic ice sheet became a pressing issue, the Chief Directorate of the Northern Sea Route, the *Glavsevmorput,* is established, the proconsulate of Otto Yulyevich Schmidt. Mathematician, geophysicist, explorer, editor-in-chief of the *Great Soviet Encyclopaedia*, this bearded colossus of Germano-Baltic origin is a friend of Alexey Feodosievich's – at least for as long as the latter remains *persona grata*. But at the time we are talking of, 1932 to 1933, he is very much *persona grata*, and is even deemed useful. Not only is he head of the weather forecasting services, but he is also chairman of the Soviet Committee for the Second International Polar Year. The ships trying to force a passage through the ice, from west to east as far as Vladivostok via the Bering Strait, are in constant communication with him, via stations positioned at intervals the length of the Siberian coast: they send him their observations and he transmits his forecasts. In 1932, the ice-breaker *Alexandr Sibiryakov* makes the first successful crossing of the Northern Sea Route without wintering. She sets sail from Arkhangelsk on the White Sea on 28 July and docks at Petropavlovsk in the Kamchatka peninsula three months later; Schmidt is the expedition leader. The following year, the steamship *Chelyuskin* puts out to sea from Leningrad in mid-July, waved off by a vast crowd on the quayside. She sails around Sweden and Norway and struggles across the Barents, Kara and Laptev seas, but is blocked by the ice field in the Chukchi Sea. She drifts and eventually sinks, her hull caving in under the pressure of the ice, on 13 February 1934.

Schmidt evacuated the entire crew, more than one hundred people including, unusually for a polar expedition, some twenty women – one even gave birth to a little girl halfway across the Kara Sea – journalists, a cameraman who filmed everything of what was to become an epic voyage, and even a Constructivist poet, Ilya Selvinsky. Schmidt organises the camp on the ice like an ideal Communist microcosm, with military discipline (anyone trying to run away, he warned, would be shot), daily saluting of the red flag to the tune of the *Internationale*, gymnastics sessions and lectures on historical materialism (given by him). They clear a landing strip, ramming down the snow, and soon, arriving from makeshift aerodromes on the Siberian coast, the drone of the first rescue planes is heard. They emerge from the blizzard and fog, skating on the ice as they land. Aviator heroes, helmeted, strapped in, booted, wearing fur-lined leather gloves and huge goggles. Bear hugs all round and everyone is crammed into the cabins in small groups. On 13 April, two months after the sinking, the evacuation is complete. They even take the sled dogs. The last to leave the camp is the captain of the *Chelyuskin*, Vladimir Ivanovich Voronin – this is not the *Costa Concordia*.

The survivors and their rescuers are given a triumphal welcome, but on a much bigger stage than Ancient Rome: crowds throng every station along the entire 9,288-kilometre length of the Trans-Siberian Railway, low-flying planes escort the train, fireboats salute them when they cross the rivers. In Moscow, they board Black Torpedoes, the procession descends Teatralny proyezd escorted by horse guards, under a shower of streamers, and on to Red Square where they are welcomed by Stalin. A gigantic parade – tanks, planes, goose-stepping regiments, and the flower of Russian youth in the white uniforms of Red athletes. What was originally a failure is transformed into a spectacular celebration of the USSR's new-found power. But Alexey Feodosievich is no longer there to see all this: fate has turned against him. While his 'friend' Schmidt is strutting around the platform of Lenin's mausoleum, beard thrust out and a flower in his buttonhole (white, curiously, not red), he has been incarcerated for two and a half months in the 'Solovki Special Purpose Camp'.

His final hour of glory was the flight of the *USSR-1* high-altitude balloon. The space race between the Soviet Union and the USA is already on, but for the time being they fly no higher than the stratosphere, going up in a balloon suspended from a huge envelope containing twenty-five cubic metres of hydrogen (smoking strictly prohibited!). The spherical gondola made of duralumin bears the letters *CCCP* (USSR). It has little portholes and a hermetically locking hatch, making it look just like a space capsule. And the launches, frequently postponed owing to adverse weather conditions, are as nail-biting as those of a shuttle (albeit less spectacular). The *USSR-1*'s maiden flight, originally scheduled for 10 September 1933, is delayed by fog and rain, and the same happens again on the 15th and 19th of that month. On the 23rd, it is decided that the launch will take place the following day. At dawn on the 24th, the military airport of Kuntsevo, to the west of Moscow, is shrouded in fog. Even so, they start inflating the 650 balloons inside the envelope held down by 150 men: the giant ectoplasm rises slowly but, saturated with moisture, it is too heavy. It wobbles at the end of its twenty-four cables and ultimately refuses to rise. During the night of the 29th, they make another attempt. The sky is clear, this time, there is no wind (the centre of the anticyclone is over Moscow), but another unforeseen problem emerges: Professor Molchanov, the designer of the instruments to be carried by the balloon and which he alone knows how to operate, hasn't arrived. The train bringing him to Leningrad has been severely delayed . . . Alexey Feodosievich spends the night studying and regulating all this fancy apparatus: precision instruments, meteorographs, barographs, altimeters, cosmic ray recorders and so on.

Thanks to him they are ready early in the morning of 30 September. At 8 a.m., the crew of three, pilot Georgy Prokofyev, Konstantin Godunov, co-pilot, and the radio operator Ernst Birnbaum, clamber into the gondola and, after a final wave, close the hatch. It is the dawn of space-hero imagery which will later feature Yuri Gagarin and Neil Armstrong and a whole army of men and soon women in white spacesuits. At 8.40, the cables are released and this time the balloon rises. Fast, even: at 9.17, Birnbaum radios to Earth that the balloon has just passed the altitude of 16,800 metres, a world record at the time. Then the rate of climb gradually decreases, and at 12.55, after Prokofyev has dumped ballast several times, *USSR-1*, now perfectly spherical, a huge, glittering ball, bombarded by sunlight in the dark blue sky, reaches the altitude of 19,500 metres. Then they descend, releasing gas, and landing without a hitch, as planned, around a hundred kilometres from their departure point near the town of Kolomna, whose population turns out en masse to watch the big flower-shaped aircraft fall out of the sky on the banks of the Moskva River. 'We congratulate the unsurpassed heroes of the stratosphere, who have brilliantly accomplished the mission entrusted to them by the Soviet authorities,' reads a telegram signed by Stalin, Molotov, Kaganovich and Voroshilov.

Heroes, the USSR has in plenty at the time – heroes of the Arctic, heroes of the stratosphere, aviators who have beaten the world long-distance record at the controls of single-engine aircraft with razor-thin wings, work heroes,

heroes building Moscow's first Metro line with its stations that are people's palaces. In 1934 the order of 'Hero of the Soviet Union' is established, and the first recipients are the search and rescue pilots of the *Chelyuskin*. There are also the unlucky heroes, the proletarian Prometheuses, such as the crew of the second high-altitude balloon, *Osoaviakhim-1*: they ascend to 22,000 metres on 30 January 1934, transmitting from up there their 'warm greetings to the great and historic Seventeenth Party Congress', which is taking place in Moscow, 'to the great and beloved Comrade Stalin and to comrades Molotov, Kaganovich and Voroshilov', but the descent goes wrong and ends up in freefall. They are given a state funeral in Red Square and monuments are built to them. (Six months later, the three Americans aboard *Explorer-1* also end up in freefall, but they manage to extricate themselves from the gondola and parachute to safety.) Over and above the hyperbole typical of Soviet rhetoric, it is indeed a time of faith in scientific and technological progress, of conviction that socialism increases its strength by serving the people, a time of passionate enthusiasms and sacrifices. 'We saw the future as an asset that indisputably belonged to us,' wrote Isaac Babel, evoking the era of the civil war, 'war as a tumultuous preparation for happiness, and happiness itself as a trait of our personality'. A phrase which beautifully encapsulates the fierce hope of the time, and which we cannot read without emotion when we recall that Babel will end up being shot at the beginning of 1940. One can't help wondering what would have happened if Stalin's madness, decapitating all the country's elites – scientific, technological, intellectual, artistic, military – decimating the peasantry and even the proletariat in whose name everything was done, whose fatherland the USSR was supposed to be, hadn't substituted terror for enthusiasm as the bedrock of Soviet life. Could the elusive 'socialism' which the 'heroes' believed they were constructing – and those too like Alexey Feodosievich Wangenheim, who weren't heroes, just honest Soviet citizens who loved their work and thought they were serving the people by doing it well – perhaps have been possible? Perhaps it would have proved a system that was infinitely preferable to capitalism? Perhaps the entire world, apart from a few backward countries, would have become socialist?

Dream on.

5

On 8 January 1934, the Commission for the Preservation of Lenin's Body had respectfully proceeded with their inspection of the embalmed Vladimir Ilich, who lay in the mausoleum in Red Square. The members of the Commission were extremely satisfied with the result: Lenin was fresh as a daisy, which represented, they stressed, 'an unprecedented scientific achievement of worldwide importance' (the pharaohs were hardly presentable). It is possible to imagine the body remaining intact indefinitely (but what the Commission had not envisaged was that the sight of the corpse of this little man with a Mongolian face, dressed in a dark suit and tie as if he were on his way to a gala dinner, would not arouse the masses indefinitely). The Commission asked Professors Vorobyov and Zbarsky, in charge of this outstanding feat of Soviet science, to write a report describing their method in detail so that the operation could be replicated in the future (whom did they have in mind?). Molotov, who countersigned the Commission's report, suggested that the two embalmers be awarded the Order of Lenin, and that they each receive the gift of 'a good car'.

One person who would not be embalmed but cremated was Andrei Bely, who had died the previous day. The Symbolist poet and brilliant and somewhat eccentric author of *Petersburg* would be accompanied to the cemetery by a group of writers including Mikhail Prishvin, Nikolay Yevreinov, Vera Inber, Boris Pilniak (who would be shot), Boris Pasternak and Osip Mandelstam (who would die in the Vladivostok transit camp). 'Infamous representative of bourgeois literature and of the idealist mentality,' wrote *Pravda*, 'in recent years, Andrei Bely sincerely sought to assimilate the ideas of socialist construction.' The last of the great exponents of Russian Symbolism, he had not shared, the paper smugly noted, 'the fate of other leaders of this literary movement (Dmitry Merezhkovsky, Zinaida Gippius, Konstantin Balmont) who sank into the swamp of the White Russian emigration: he died a Soviet writer'. Bely's real name was Boris Bugayev, and he was the son of the mathematician chancellor who, in 1901, had expelled Alexey Feodosievich from Moscow University.

In all other respects, that 8 January was a normal Soviet day. Work heroes and saboteurs played opposite one another. *Izvestiya* announced that the 1933 harvests had beaten all records, thanks to the Party's far-sighted policy which had prevailed over the kulaks' sabotage and boosted the development of the kolkhozes and of mechanisation (and caused the appalling famine in Ukraine, but that escaped *Izvestiya*). Improved mechanisation, maybe, but tractors were still a problem. Admittedly, the 50,000th tractor, named 'Seventeenth Congress', rolled off the Kharkov factory production line; admittedly, but in the meantime, at the maintenance centre in Tajikistan, workers were twiddling their thumbs, fulfilling only 0.3 per cent of the plan. That's right, 0.3 per cent. For a much less serious shortfall, the manager of the Yaroslavl rubber plant was fired while waiting to be rehabilitated through work: set a target of 9,000 tyres by the production plan, the impudent dog had declared on 23 December that this was not achievable. Not achievable. 'The plan set by the Government is a law,' retorted *Pravda*; 'to oppose it is a violation of Party discipline and Soviet law.' Alas, the deplorable Mikhaylov (as the sabotaging manager was called) was not the only one to put a surreptitious spoke in the wheels of socialism; the tractor maintenance workshops of central Asia had to send back 3,000 weak connecting rod bearings, 1,049 pistons manufactured at Plant Number Seventeen which were the wrong size, and as for the segments from the Frunze plant in Penza, they were all faulty. And what about the Skorokhod ('Walk Fast') shoe factory in Leningrad which had to return 16,000 pairs of soles from Promtekhnika? When it emerged that Promtekhnika produced precisely 16,000 pairs of soles a day, that meant the factory had worked for an entire day for nothing. Who were they kidding?

And on the saboteurs' side there was still Comrade (for how much longer?) Russanov, director of the Moscow–White Sea railway (which Alexey Feodosievich would soon travel, in a cattle truck), who complained of not having enough rolling stock when he had more than enough. The thing was, he allowed shirkers to thrive, so the trains were never ready to leave. And Comrade, or soon ex-Comrade Zhukov, director of the Western Railway, was in the same situation. As was the head of the Southern Railway, who delayed the loading of coal from the Donbass mines. And then there were the good-for-nothings from the Perm power plant, who from the beginning of winter disrupted production with ill-timed power cuts.

Luckily there were the heroes, the shock workers. The kolkhoz zealots and workers on the 'Prozhektor' kolkhoz who promised to work even harder and better. The activists building the Metro who, assembled by Comrade Kaganovich, pledged to finish building the first line in time for the seventeenth anniversary of the October Revolution. The Adzhariya kolkhoz and sovkhoz workers who dispatched seventeen wagons of clementines, oranges and lemons as a gift to the delegates attending the Seventeenth Congress and to the workers of Moscow. The shock teams of women workers from twenty-five Leningrad factories sent a declaration of love to Stalin:

Great master, our best friend, dear Comrade Stalin,
The past is erased for ever!
We have always been with the Bolsheviks,
The woman worker's consciousness has been
    raised high beyond recognition.

Life grows richer and more and more beautiful.
We want to work as hard as possible, accomplish
    all the tasks to the best of our ability.
Comrade Stalin! You have made our country
    invincible.

And the proof that life was getting better and richer all the time was the shop Gastronom, at the corner of Tverskaya Street and Bolshoy Gnezdnikovsky pereulok in Moscow (just one example), which a report showed groaning under the weight of sausages from Kraków and Poltava, strings of sausages, hams, 'the finest specimens from the Black Sea, the Sea of Azov and the Barents Sea as well as of the Soviet rivers', herring from Kerch, salmon, sturgeon, pike perch, mullet, and so on. It was a real symphony, which quite understandably reminded the *Pravda* journalist, a man of letters and poetry, of the descriptions in Zola's *The Belly of Paris*. The first television set, the TK-1 model, was made at the Kozitsky factory in Leningrad, the production of electric gramophones was beginning, red flags fluttered above the Communist Youth International factory to celebrate the launch of sewing-machine-needle production, twenty-one bicycles made in the factories of Moscow, Kharkov and Penza were about to set off on a 1,200-kilometre race along the Black Sea coast to test the quality of the equipment. The agitprop squad of the paramilitary organisation Osoaviakhim had taken off from Kharkov for Stalino oblast, in the Donbass region.

Maybe Alexey Feodosievich glanced distractedly at this latest news, unaware that this issue 5894 of *Pravda* was the last he would buy from a kiosk (or perhaps he had it delivered to his office?); the last, in any case, of his life as a free man. Did he recall now the malicious Nikolay Bugayev, father of Bely, who, thirty-three years earlier had fired him from Moscow University where Alexey himself now teaches physics? A great mathematician, all the same, that Bugayev. Perhaps he'd read, stifling a yawn, the story of the manager of the Yaroslavl rubber plant, or perhaps with indignation, who knows, unaware that the next day he would also be a saboteur and a Soviet outlaw. Unaware that this issue of *Pravda* was the last of the era when he was known as Comrade Alexey Feodosievich Wangenheim, director of the unified Hydro-meteorological Department of the USSR, chairman of the Hydro-meteorological Committee of the Council of People's Commissars, head of the Weather Bureau, chairman of the Soviet Committee for the Organisation of the Second Polar Year, and numerous other titles? Of the time when he was called simply Comrade?

I imagine – but I could be wrong – that he paid scant attention to all those stories of tractors, sewing-machine needles and succulent sausages. Not that he wasn't a good Communist, but his field of expertise was clouds, winds, rains, isobars, the ice sheets of the Northern Sea Route. His role in the construction of socialism was to help the revolutionary proletariat control the forces of Nature. Each person to their work station, their battle station: he was an organised man. Did the story of the professors opening up Vladimir Ilich to see if he'd gone off make him smile? I don't think so, I can't imagine him showing any inclination to disrespect. I'd like to, but somehow I don't think so, unfortunately. Did he take an interest in international news, then? From London, there were cables expressing growing concern for the fate of Georgy Dimitrov, still held prisoner by the German government even though he had been found not guilty of the charge of setting fire to the Reichstag. From Paris, the TASS agency wired that the former president of the Chamber of Deputies, Édouard Herriot was on a lecture tour of the South of France to extol the achievements of Soviet industry and agriculture. (Herriot had been shown all over the devastated Ukraine in 1933, but of course he had only seen happy kolkhoz workers feasting beneath portraits of Stalin, which permitted him to 'shrug' when anyone spoke to him of famine. Grossman alludes to Herriot's visit in *Everything Flows*: in the heart of the Dnipropetrovsk region, where cannibalism was rife, he was taken to a kolkhoz crèche, and he asked the children what they'd had for lunch that day. 'Chicken soup, *pirozhki* and rice croquettes,' came the answer. Herriot was less perceptive than André Gide – sometimes writers are better judges of world affairs than politicians.) There was also the scandal still referred to as 'the Crédit municipal de Bayonne affair', an ingenious swindle carried out by an embezzler called Alexandre Stavisky. Correspondence dated 7 January mentioned his countless relations among the French ruling class. As Alexey Feodosievich was perhaps skimming this article, 'the handsome Sasha' was found dying in a chalet in Chamonix, having committed 'suicide with a bullet from a revolver fired point blank' – but the readers of *Pravda* would only learn of this the following day. The article of 8 January was the first of a serial, the rest of which the meteorologist would never know, although it probably did not interest him greatly. Perhaps he might infer a few vague considerations from it (or rather confirmations of his beliefs) about the corruption of the capitalist world and the inevitable victory of socialism (etc.).

In the Far East, Japan was tightening its grip on North China, and was preparing to make the weak Puyi 'the last emperor'. Imprisoned in Shanghai, the Comintern agents Paul Ruegg and Gertrude Noulens, real names Yakov Rudnik and Tatyana Moiseenko and not at all Swiss as shown on their passports, were on their nineteenth day of hunger strike, and their lives were in danger. Telegrams of protest poured in from around the world, and especially Paris, to the Chinese embassies or of what remained of China (this was straight out of *The Human Condition,* André Malraux's novel that had just won the Prix Goncourt). In Harbin, in the north of Manchuria under Japanese occupation, the tortured body of a young French pianist had been discovered. The unfortunate Simon Kaspé, son of a wealthy Jewish businessman in the city, had been kidnapped three months earlier, when he had come to visit his family, by a gang of henchmen of the Russian fascist party who demanded a ransom of 100,000 dollars. They had cut off his ears, among other acts of torture. The Japanese police had made no effort to track them down (and when they were arrested, they were pardoned by the emperor).

In those days, there was no weather forecast in *Pravda*. Was that because it wasn't considered useful? Had Alexey Feodosievich asked in vain to be given a regular column in the organ of the Central Committee? I don't know. It was an austere paper, as one would expect, with a single photo illustrating the manufacture of sewing-machine needles, which was not a very photogenic subject. If there had been a weather bulletin, it would have said something like a vast anticyclone with central pressure of 1,045 millibars, directly over the Urals, would result in the arrival of very warm air over the west of the country and cause heavy snowfall from Karelia in the north to Mordovia in the south. Conversely it would bring very cold temperatures with a clear sky over the far east, from the West Siberian kray (region) to the Pacific coast. The next day, little change: heavy snowfall expected over the Moscow region and the Volga, while the entire east would continue to have dry weather with temperatures of −20 to −30 degrees. But the next day . . . Two further articles must certainly have caught Alexey Feodosievich's eye for a moment, if he had time that day to read *Pravda:* Ilya Selvinsky, the Futurist poet, had sent news over the wireless that the *Chelyuskin* had begun drifting again on the Arctic Ocean heading in a south-easterly direction, whereas during December it had been moving northwards. A violent north-easterly wind had broken up the ice field, piling up blocks several metres high. The ice was compressing the ship's hull, which for the moment was holding out. All the same, measures had been taken in readiness for an evacuation, with provisions and tents stored on the deck. Schmidt thought of everything. The scientific research went on. And then, a second little article: Kliment Voroshilov had informed Stalin that the preparations had begun for the flight of the high-altitude balloon *Osoaviakhim-1* at the Kuntsevo airfield. The crew of three, Pavel Fedoseenko, Andrey Vasenko and Ilya Usyskin, were ready. Their goal was to set a new world record to mark the Seventeenth Party Congress, which would open in Moscow on 26 January. But Alexey Feodosievich already knew all that.

6

On the evening of 8 January 1934, it is snowing over Moscow. The red stars shine in the purple sky, the towers and crenellated walls the colour of dried blood truly make the Kremlin 'a habitation that would suit some of the personages of the Apocalypse', as it was described by the celebrated nineteenth-century French traveller, the Marquis de Custine. The occasional black car cruises slowly down the wide, white avenues, trams send out flashes, and pedestrians hurry along the pavements, collars turned up, fur hats pulled down. Chasms are opening in Moscow's soil: the giant hole left on the riverbank by the destruction of the Cathedral of Christ the Saviour, the access shafts to the underground building works for Moscow's first Metro line sending up columns of smoke. Alexey Feodosievich has bought tickets for the Bolshoi's evening performance of *Sadko*, an opera by Rimsky-Korsakov that recounts the underwater adventures of the wealthy merchant Sadko with the Sea King's daughter. He has arranged to meet his wife under the colonnade in front of the theatre. She waits for him in vain; the last stragglers have long since gone inside, shaking the snow from their coats, removing their galoshes. The bell rings and still he doesn't come. The snow streaks the purple haloes around the red stars on top of the Kremlin's towers. He will not come; right now he is not far from the Bolshoi, barely a few hundred metres away, but separated from his wife by a vast distance, in a world from which it is much harder to return than from Sadko's underwater world: a 'penalty isolator' cell in the Lubyanka, the GPU's headquarters.

I do not know whether Alexey Feodosievich had felt the menace closing in, but I imagine he had – unless he was utterly blinded by his Communist faith. As the son of a noble and brother of an émigré, he was in any case a natural candidate for the suspicions of the paranoid secret police. For some time, the noose had been tightening around him. And not only him – the reality of the terror Stalin was beginning to impose was that no one was spared, no matter how high up they were, no matter how faithfully they executed their menial task. No one was exempt from the threat of death. The NKVD investigators who will interrogate him will themselves end up close by, interrogated in turn and then shot, likewise the dreaded Genrikh Yagoda, the People's Commissar for Internal Affairs, in charge of the Lubyanka. And so the net was closing in not only on those around him, but also on him. In March 1933, an allegedly counter-revolutionary organisation made up of individuals 'of bourgeois origin and major landowners' had been discovered within the People's Commissariat of Land Cultivation, under the aegis of which Alexey Feodosievich's department came. Thirty-five 'conspirators' were shot, along with their leader, Moses Wolfe. And then there were venomous articles by Nikolay Nikolayevich Speransky even though he was one of Wangenheim's subordinates.

Wangenheim had helped introduce into Soviet meteorological circles the 'Norwegian theory' – in a nutshell a theory that cyclones originated from undulations when a polar front comes into contact with a warm front. One of the originators of this theory, which would be widely espoused in the twentieth century, the Swede (despite his name) Bergeron, had been invited to lecture in the USSR; articles were published in specialist journals, in particular one by a young colleague in the Weather Bureau, Sergey Khromov, entitled 'New ideas in meteorology and their philosophical implications'. 'New ideas' – really? That is what gave rise to suspicion. As if Marx–Engels–Lenin–Stalin were not sufficient, and didn't have the answers to everything ... Speransky accused the scatterbrain of omitting to make reference to Lenin ('it seems unbelievable that a person can forget Lenin by accident'); worse still, of not citing Stalin's works as recommended reading! He urged the 'firm rejection of foreign class propaganda concealed under Marxist disguise'. And in another article he thundered against 'the heap of rubbish deliberately spread by enemy hands' and a 'Menshevist tendency evident in the press of the hydro-meteorological department'. Omission of Lenin and Stalin, foreign class propaganda, a Menshevist tendency: these were terrible words in the USSR of the time, and particularly the one that was emerging – words that kill. Wangenheim is fully aware that it is he, Khromov's boss and editor of the journal who is responsible for publishing this 'heap of rubbish', who is the target. He underlines the most damning passages in red.

Finally, in November 1933, one of his close colleagues at the Central Weather Bureau, Mikhail Loris-Melikov, is arrested in Leningrad. Under interrogation, he spills the beans, claims there is a clandestine counter-revolutionary organisation within the Hydro-meteorological Department, headed by Professor Wangenheim who is 'of an authoritarian and careerist temperament, politically hostile to the Party'. The purpose of the conspiracy: to sabotage the battle against drought by disrupting the weather station network and falsifying the forecasts (this is the first time that incorrect weather forecasts can result in death). And Loris-Melikov grasses not only on his boss, but on other colleagues, including a certain Ivan Ivanovich Kramaley, of noble birth, like himself (and having, like Wangenheim, an émigré brother serving in the French Foreign Legion). So Kramaley is arrested, and he confirms Loris-Melikov's statement and adds further names. Now there is enough evidence in the file of the GPU bloodhounds for them to proceed with Wangenheim's arrest.

The only person detained who informs on no one and denies all the accusations is Gavril Nazarov, not a Party member and of peasant stock. Although he has a heart condition and is highly strung, he stands up to the GPU men. I do not mention this to assert the superiority of peasant stock over noble blood, but primarily to pay a belated tribute to his solitary courage, and then to raise the eternal question of Stalinist trials: why did the accused, whether important dignitaries or petty officials, marshals, Companions of Lenin, founders of the Bolshevik Party, or humble meteorologists, end up admitting to the trumped-up crimes they were accused of by the secret police? Apparently torture, which will be commonplace during the Great Terror of 1937 to 1938, is not routinely used in 1933–1934: we're still in the phase of 'ordinary' terror. But there are the beatings, humiliations and threats to families, whom those arrested desperately hope to protect by telling the interrogators what they want to hear. There is the exhaustion caused by days and nights without sleep with non-stop interrogations by alternating teams who relentlessly ask the same questions over and over again, formulated slightly differently, heard in a state of semi-consciousness. There is the mental breakdown caused by suddenly being treated as an enemy of the people, when they are used to thinking of the entire world as a Manichaean battle between the people and its enemies, which nothing can escape; there is their faith in the Party which they desperately cling to through thick and thin, their irrational trust in their leaders and in the greatest, the most far-seeing, the most humane of them all . . . All these reasons are pure supposition – ultimately we know nothing. A person who has not experienced that horror is not capable of making the journey in their imagination.

The fact is, Gavril Nazarov did not confess, did not testify against the others. He was sentenced to five years of prison camp under article 58 of the Criminal Code of the Socialist Republic of Russia, paragraph 7, punishing economic sabotage. I do not know where or how he died, but I am certain that it wasn't in his bed. Mikhail Loris-Melikov died in 1936 in a labour camp in Ukhta. The two GPU officers who had signed his indictment, Derenik Apressian and Alexandr Chanin, were shot, one in 1939 and the other in 1937. The head of the GPU, Genrikh Yagoda, who had signed the arrest warrant for Loris-Melikov and other 'saboteurs', was shot in March 1938, after pleading guilty (in particular) to having poisoned Maxim Gorky. It is a tale, told by an idiot, full of sound and fury, signifying nothing … .

So, it is 8 January 1934. Arrest and search warrant no. 14234 is delivered by Yagoda's deputy, Georgy Prokofyev (who has the same name as the pilot of the *USSR-1* high-altitude balloon, and will be shot in 1937). The search is conducted at Alexey Feodosievich's office and at his home, 7 Dokuchayev pereulok. During my last stay in Moscow, I went to see whether the building was still there, and it was – one of the few not to have been demolished, not far from the vast Sukharevskaya Avenue, Three Stations Square and the Stalinist skyscrapers of the Hotel Leningrad and the Ministry of Heavy Industry (which didn't exist back then). The small, cream-coloured neoclassical building is reached through a porch, with one storey looking out on to the street and two overlooking the courtyard, and is now home to the Children's Music School of V. F. Odoevsky. A few reedy piano notes can be heard coming from the first floor; in the courtyard kids are having fun sliding on the ice (it's December, as attested by the blue fairy lights of the modest Christmas decorations). It is strange to think that the cruel story I'm telling today, eighty years on, began in this peaceful house dedicated to music – it is strange, but what Moscow house has not witnessed terrible things?

7

The huge Lubyanka edifice, an eight-storey fortress, more or less trapezoid in shape built around deep court-yards, was the headquarters of the secret police, which often changed its name – originally called the Cheka it then became the GPU (GPU, which meant State Political Directorate) or OGPU, if an O is added for *Obedinyonnoye*, 'United'. The GPU then merged, in July 1934, with the NKVD, the People's Commissariat for Internal Affairs. No matter what name it went under, the Lubyanka was equally as brutal. It was also a prison and a place where executions were carried out. The entire process was conducted within its walls, from interrogation through to execution of the sentence, which took place in the vaults. The convicts, dressed only in their underwear (death was not enough, humiliation was also required), were taken into a room whose floor was covered in tarpaulin and there they were killed with a shot in the back of the neck, usually from a short-barrel 7.62 Nagant revolver. Then the tarpaulin was scrubbed down; there was a concern for hygiene on every floor of the Lubyanka. For example it was there, in the basements, that Zinovyev and Kamenev would be executed, after the first Moscow show trial. But above all, so many others too, whose names have been forgotten.

You cannot gaze without emotion, without that sense of awe inspired by places of horror, at the Lubyanka's imposing grey and ochre façade with its bands of rose-coloured cornices, dominating the square of its namesake, on exiting the Metro station of the same name. I say 'you', but who, in fact? Those for whom revolutionary hope and its dire death mattered in one way or another at some point in their lives. Because if there is a place that symbolises the mass murder of the ideal, the gruesome substitution of terror for enthusiasm, of police officers for comrades, it is the Lubyanka. This is the home of the reverse alchemy that transformed gold into worthless lead. How many thousands of free and courageous men and women came out of that slaughterhouse broken, slaves? I certainly don't idealise Communism, but I also know the hope it represented, the tremendous force it set in motion. How many thousands were murdered in the cellars of this huge bourgeois building, with its ornate Italianate style, that was originally the head office of the All-Russia Insurance Company? This emotion, this awe, does not seem to affect many in Moscow. The numerous pedestrians in the square pay no special attention to this infamous monument. A residue of fear, perhaps? The only plaque on the walls states that here Yury Andropov was head of the KGB from 1967 to 1982. Nothing about the many martyrs who had a bullet through their heads a few floors below Yury Andropov's office. All around the Lubyanka are the luxury stores of the new Russia, the perfumeries, jewellers, Gucci boutiques and Ferrari showrooms with hostesses teetering on stiletto heels and guarded by heavies in black tracksuits.

An empty room, harshly lit. A man in a white coat. Get undressed. Turn around. Bend over. Spread your legs. The stay in the Lubyanka begins with a body search. The naked prisoner, prodded, poked, humiliated, has definitively ceased to be a comrade. 'Even when for months one has become accustomed to the idea of being in prison,' wrote Margarete Buber-Neumann, the wife of the German Communist leader Heinz Neumann, who was deported by Stalin then handed over by him to Hitler, 'you learn when you sit for the first time behind a locked door without a handle; and a bodily search at the Lubyanka is the thing to let you know to the full what it is to be a prisoner; not even the most intimate parts of your body are any longer your own.' After the search, prisoners get dressed again, in clothes whose buttons have been pulled off. They walk down endless corridors bathed in a harsh light, holding up their trousers with both hands, an armed guard behind them. Fingerprints, photos. Mugshots of 'Wangenheim Al-ey F', showing him looking straight ahead and in profile, stamped with the number 34776. His face is heavy, his gaze blank, or expressing a gloomy bewilderment. Not the expression of pure panic or despondency that makes some photos of NKVD convicts so hard to look at. It is the same face as in the photo with him wearing a tie, but suddenly aged, subdued. Bundled up in a dark coat.

They walk down endless corridors smelling of disinfectant, then he is pushed into a tiny, overheated, windowless cell, nicknamed 'the dog kennel', *sobachnik*: he's become a dog. He waits, is taken out, they go up in a lift, walk down more corridors carpeted in red like in a hotel, red warning lights to indicate that they are not likely to meet another prisoner, he's shoved into an office where the GPU investigators are waiting, Alexandr Chanin and Leonid Gazov. They both belong to the Economic section, in charge of punishing crimes against Soviet agriculture and industry. The former will be shot in 1937 and the latter will die, honoured and decorated, fifty years later: life is unfair. Chanin will even be shot two and a half months before Wangenheim, which he is certainly far from suspecting, that 8 January when, calm and frosty, professional, he takes down identity details from the dazed enemy of the people clutching his trousers with both hands. It is a tale, told by an idiot ... Surname, patronymic, first name, born in Krapivno, Socialist Republic of Ukraine, former noble and landowner, former officer in the Tsar's army, former director of the Hydro-meteorological Department, former member of the Bolshevik Communist Party of the Soviet Union ... Alexey Feodosievich is nothing but the annihilation of what he was, a void like the one left in the landscape by the destruction of the Cathedral of Christ the Saviour in Moscow. He has not yet been informed of his new social identity as a saboteur and spy. Then he is taken to a solitary cell, with the lights permanently on, where he is watched at regular intervals through the spyhole. He is in the OGPU 'penalty isolator'.

Some prisoners are left to stew for weeks without knowing what they are accused of, but he is lucky, so to speak: he only has to wait five days before being summoned to his first interrogation. Chanin is no longer there, replaced by Derenik Apressian, partnered with Gazov. They are clean and close-shaven in their blue-trimmed uniforms. I picture them aloof, calm, never raising their voices. They have all the time in the world. They flick through a file that contains, as Wangenheim soon realises, alongside false testimonies by Loris-Melikov and Kramaley, a large amount of correct information about him, apparently insignificant details but which cumulatively make it seem as if Apressian and Gazov know everything and it is pointless to try and dupe them. I imagine they affect an air of indifferent patience – sharpening a pencil, lighting a cigarette, buffing their nails or telephoning their wives or mistresses – while he desperately racks his brains and tries to grasp what they are driving at, what answer he should give in order to be believed, not to contradict himself, snared in the web of their insidious questions, their tranquil hostility (but maybe on the contrary, they are rough from the start). From the outset they disconcert him by producing a note, found at his home during the search, in which a man named Gudyakov reports the words of Vitold Vitkevich, a meteorology professor at the Agrarian Academy, alleging that Alexey was 'a dangerous element who would one day have to account for himself as a saboteur'. Did he agree with that assessment? No, clearly not. So why had he not taken steps against that slanderer? 'Out of stupidity.' Had he tried to clarify the reasons for this accusation? No, he had considered it merely an expression of Vitkevich's rancour and had not been worried by it. Did he know that there were in fact charges against Vitkevich? Yes, he had been informed of them. Had he passed this information on to the OGPU? No. Why not? He assumed that the person who had told him would pass it on himself. Had he checked that this had been done? No. Did he think that was right? No, now he realises that was a mistake. From the start of this affair, although he has shown humanity, indifference to slander and has refused to inform, he is in the position of having lied by omission to those to whom everything must be reported because it is their job to know and hear everything.

And a little later, he is to put himself in an even worse situation by retracting his initial declarations in writing. In fact he only discovered the contents of Gudyakov's note on 13 January, during the interrogation, which threw him off balance. He hadn't had the time to read that note, he'd been very busy when it was passed on to him, he'd vaguely seen that it was to do with Vitkevich's misdemeanours, then he'd stuffed it into a drawer and forgotten about it. The fly struggles and becomes further enmeshed in the web, under the gaze of the two GPU spiders. Who then grill him about his attitude during the civil war. Apressian and Gazov are surprised, or pretend to be, that he stayed in the Dmitriev region when the Whites took the city. Why then, when he was asked if he had been with the Whites, had he replied no? Because he'd understood the question in the sense of 'did you fight on their side?' How could he prove that he hadn't tried to hide the fact that he'd remained in White territory? But he had mentioned it in his curriculum vitae when he'd applied to join the Party, in 1924 ... He had hidden in the Dmitriev area, at the home of a peasant called Bardin whom he had known since 1910. And what were this peasant's political opinions? Neither White nor Red, politically indifferent. So how can he explain why Bardin took the risk of hiding him? Because he knew him and was fond of him. It is clear that the notion of fondness means little to the two men with blue epaulettes. Or even that it clearly reeks of Menshevism. And why had he not attempted to get to the region controlled by the Reds? Because his wife, his first wife, Yuliya Bolotova, was ill in Dmitriev, and he didn't want to be separated from her by the front line. Really, was it for such an unimportant reason that he hadn't joined the Reds? He does not think that his wife's illness is an unimportant reason. The two raise their eyebrows and the corners of their mouths turn down in contempt. Do you admit, they ask him, to bring this interrogation to a close, that the nature of your answers from 17 January does not inspire confidence? I refuse to reply to a question formulated in that way, he retorts. He is not yet ready to accept the entire thing, not yet crushed.

But three weeks later, on 9 February, he is. Apressian and Gazov have done a good job. On 20 January, they presented him with the charges: organising and leading counter-revolutionary sabotage work in the USSR's Hydrometeorological Department, including knowingly fabricating false weather forecasts with the aim of damaging socialist agriculture, and the disruption or destruction of the weather station network, especially the stations designed to prevent droughts; on top of these accusations they added, for good measure, collecting secret data for espionage purposes. On 20 January, he does not plead guilty. But on 9 February, like so many others before and particularly after him, he signs a long and terrible confession that opens with the following preamble: 'Taking into account my sincere remorse and my regret at having acted criminally against the Party, the Soviet leadership and the working class, I hope in the future, if I am allowed to live, to expiate my guilt fully through honest and intensive labour for the good of the Soviet Union, and I declare the following.' This way of evoking the threat of death himself, of accepting it as a foregone conclusion, as justified – 'if I am allowed to live' – is chilling. If they will be so good as to let me out of here alive . . .

He admits to having led the counter-revolutionary sabotage organisation within the Hydro-meteorological Department, the aim of which was to hinder the development of socialist agriculture. He says he was recruited by Moses Wolfe, which at least avoided compromising anyone else since Wolfe had already been shot, in 1933. His detailed confession is interesting on this point: 'Having understood,' he wrote, 'that I did not agree with the Party's agricultural policy, especially with the severe dekulakisation of those I do not consider to be kulaks, Wolfe told me that there was a counter-revolutionary organisation . . .' Bearing in mind that the executions and deportations resulting from dekulakisation amounted to millions, it is to be hoped and believed that on that matter Wangenheim's confession is sincere. He then gives (or rather the GPU's 'investigators' dictate to him) numerous details of his alleged sabotage activities, all aimed at depriving agriculture of the means to forecast the weather, droughts in particular. It is clearly vital to find scapegoats for the catastrophic harvests and the resulting human disaster.

The espionage charges are being investigated at the same time. In this instance, the accuser is Pavel Vasilyev, a member of the Leningrad Hydrology Department, who claims to have been recruited to provide intelligence on the aerodromes of the frontier region and the forts guarding Kronstadt's sea approaches. This Vasilyev is extremely talkative and reveals a great deal about artillery calibres and the names of alleged informers. And now, on 23 February, in an address to the Prosecutor, and again on 17 March, in a memorandum addressed to the OGPU's judiciary collegium body, Wangenheim retracts his confessions. The testimonies of Loris-Melikov, Kramaley and Vasilyev, he writes, are false testimonies, giving credence to the myth of a counter-revolutionary organisation which did not in fact exist. They had been 'coerced by the interrogation method': unfortunately, he does not elaborate, and his style is so convoluted that it is difficult today to get a clear idea (but doubtless the senior OGPU officials understood that language perfectly, and doubtless they were able to decipher the rhetorical effects of fear: the prisoner wants to protest against the way he has been treated, but dares not do so too openly. He tacitly accuses his interrogators, while heaping ritual praise on the secret police they are part of; it's what is called contortions). The interrogation methods 'have unquestionably achieved outstanding results for which the OGPU is renowned', says Wangenheim, not one 'erroneous page' should ruin that. On the contrary, that 'erroneous page should be replaced by a glorious new page demonstrating the OGPU's infallibility'. But, 'each day with the current methods and each new confrontation tighten the knot of lies a little more, despite the commitment and conscientiousness of those leading the investigation'.

To be honest, these poorly written and poorly argued retractions are redolent of panic, not only and probably not even initially the understandable panic at the thought of the fate awaiting him – death or deportation – but also and above all the intellectual panic he is thrown into by the fact that the more he plays the lying game, the more credible he is, while the truth becomes less and less so, the moral panic he experiences on realising that admitting his guilt can earn him relative indulgence, whereas insisting on his innocence will condemn him (here another quotation from Shakespeare comes to mind: the witches in *Macbeth*'s 'fair is foul and foul is fair'). And yet he proclaims his innocence anew, retracting his false confessions. 'For a real culprit, this kind of step can only be explained by idiocy or madness.' When he challenges 'the interrogation method', I believe he means this perversion in particular: mental rather than physical brutality, the agonising reversal of the true and the false. That is what makes these writings so moving: we see a man becoming further and further mired in quicksand the more he struggles. And all the same, alongside a lot of confusion, meanders and tentative repetitions, there are phrases we are not accustomed to reading in the Soviet documents of those years, which show that he definitely does not fit the role of repentant saboteur and spy they want him to play, which he agreed to in a moment of weakness: 'In most cases, the innocent people arrested make false confessions', 'inevitably there are many cases where innocent people have been charged whereas the true criminals escape justice'. Moving too is his awareness that the game is probably lost: 'It is very possible that I have insufficient strength to defeat the order of things established years ago.' And he concludes in Latin: *Feci quod potui, faciant meliora potentes*, 'I have done what I could, let those who can do better' (words spoken by Kulygin, Masha's husband in Chekhov's *Three Sisters*). 'My conscience is clean.'

He did what he could, but he could do nothing; the game was lost in any case. The fact was, there was no game, the outcome was a foregone conclusion. On 27 March, the OGPU's judiciary collegium reviewing case no. 3039, that of the accused Wangenheim, former noble, charged under article 58, paragraphs 6 (espionage) and 7 (economic sabotage), Kramaley, former noble, Loris-Melikov, former noble, and Nazarov, son of a kulak, charged under article 58, paragraph 7, determines that under article 58.7 Wangenheim be sentenced to ten years' rehabilitation through labour. Investigation of offence 58.6 is postponed. Kramaley, Loris-Melikov and Nazarov each receive five years.

8

Now that Wangenheim is to leave Moscow for ever, because the remainder and the end of this story, his story, will take place in a small region in the north-west of Russia, east of Finland, let us try to sketch out the map in words. In the easternmost corner of the Baltic, Leningrad. Some five hundred kilometres to the north-east, below the Arctic Circle, the White Sea, which is like a vast, almost enclosed inlet of the Barents Sea. On the east coast, Arkhangelsk, in the centre, the Solovetsky Islands, on the west coast, the little town of Kem. On the isthmus between the two seas, two big lakes, Ladoga and Onega, crossed by the White Sea–Baltic canal. On the shores of Lake Onega, to the very north, the town of Medvezhegorsk, 'capital' of the *BelBaltLag*, the canal camp complex; a little further south Petrozavodsk, capital of the Socialist Republic of Karelia. Its landscape corrugated by glacial erosion, with lakes dotted everywhere and covered by forests. It is a blood-soaked land, strewn with the dead: the dead from the many concentration camps built there, those shot during the Great Terror of 1937 to 1938, which was particularly savage in this frontier region that was ethnically non-Russian and so doubly suspect, those killed in the Russo-Finnish wars between 1939 and 1944, and the ensuing wave of purges.

9

On 8 May 1934, four months to the day after his arrest, convict Alexey Feodosievich Wangenheim is part of a convoy destined for the *Solovetsky lager osobogo naznacheniya* (SLON) – the 'Solovki Special Purpose Camp'. The day before, his wife is given permission to visit him in the Lubyanka. This is the first time she has seen him since that snowy day when she waited in vain for him under the colonnade of the Bolshoi. It is also the last. Varvara Ivanovna brings a photo of their daughter Eleonora, named after Marx's daughter and not yet four. 'You came into my life like a little bright sun,' he writes to Varvara on his arrival at the Kem transit camp on the 11th, 'and it is always before me.' He calculates that he will be released in 1944, at the age of sixty-two . . .

The Solovki camp is considered to be the first Gulag forced labour camp, but that is not entirely true: camps had been opened in the Arkhangelsk region (Kholmogory, Pertominsk) before the Cheka expelled the monks from the Solovetsky monastery in 1923, leaving a fire in their wake, and then establishing the SLON there. Even though the camps were horrifically expanded under Stalin, they were an inevitable early consequence of Leninism. But the Solovki camp out-shone its rivals, so to speak, perhaps because of its powerful holy associations – the monastery was one of the major Russian pilgrimage sites – and in particular it was the birthplace of the idea that the constantly growing mass of deportees should serve the Soviet Union's fanatical industrialisation drive. It was here that the training techniques for exploiting this immense workforce to death were developed. During the 1920s, prisoners from all over Russia were brought to the islands; from the beginning of the thirties, while they continued to arrive in convoys, others left, contingents of slaves sent to work on the USSR's large-scale projects – the Vorkuta and Norilsk coal mines, the logging camps in Karelia, and primarily the construction of the deadly BBK, the *Belomorsko-Baltiysky kanal*, the White Sea–Baltic Canal. 'And the archipelago,' wrote Solzhenitsyn, was 'born and came to maturity on Solovki': a coincidence that made the geographical Solovetsky Islands archipelago the matrix for the metaphorical Gulag archipelago. The lock through which this human tide passed was the Kem transit camp on the Karelian coast: it was the departure point for the islands, the place where people waited when the sea was frozen for ships to resume sailing, and it was also the landing stage from where the *zeks* – the prisoners – were dispatched to labour camps in the north of Russia.

It was generally a three- or four-day train journey from Moscow to Kem (but it could take twice as long). I imagine him crammed into a goods wagon with around a hundred others, as is customary. One of those wagons which the so-called Comrade Rusanov complained of not having in sufficient quantities, according to *Pravda* on the date of Wangenheim's arrest . . . But for this particular train, these particular goods – men, women, human equipment – they certainly found the wagons they needed. All his possessions are tied up in a large handkerchief to prevent them from being stolen by common thieves, the political prisoners' sworn enemies and bugbear. Being fleeced by the *urkas* – the thugs, the underworld – is an almost unavoidable initiation into the camp. Like everyone else, he is given a ration of dried fish and black bread. He has no cup from which to drink the hot water, and perhaps a fellow prisoner lends him one. And for shitting, there's a stinking pail in the middle of the wagon, which they empty at the stops, when permitted by the escort. The former noble and former comrade will have to get used to it. But perhaps instead he travels in a 'Stolypin' cell wagon, named after Nicholas II's prime minister. It can hardly be described as luxurious, but even so it is a little less terrible than the pure and simple cattle wagon – it is deportation *Ancien Régime* style. If he does, he will be able to glimpse through the barred windows, as Yevgeniya Ginzburg describes in *Journey into the Whirlwind*, each little station in Moscow's suburbs, decorated with red banners printed with anti-'saboteur' slogans . . .

Nowadays, the Moscow–Murmansk *Arktika* express takes exactly twenty-four hours to reach Kem, in the dead of night. It is a very comfortable train, which tends to be slow, like all Russian trains, but this slowness has a certain charm: it allows you to gaze at leisure at the landscape of forests and lakes glittering with a riot of golds, purples and mauves in the interminable dusk glow of spring. The *provodnitsa* – carriage attendant – is a plump, smiling mother figure, which is far from usual. Despite the jolts, she diligently embroiders a pattern of a languorous kiss in the centre of a lace doily. My fellow traveller, a tall, gangly, fair-haired oaf with a childlike smile, a border guard between Murmansk and Kirkenes, generously shares the *viski* in his hip flask. Pitching up in Kem at one o'clock in the morning is a bit like arriving beyond the end of the world. The daylight does nothing to fundamentally change that impression. Kem is a faded little town on the estuary of the river of the same name. There is a very beautiful tumbledown wooden church. Nowadays the former OGPU headquarters houses a huge, rather sinister cafe, but all the same it's more pleasant than before. The site of the transit camp is some twenty kilometres away, at Rabocheostrovsk, 'Workers Island'. Dilapidated *izbas* log huts and boats rotting on the shore, between cabins and rusty tanks. The fishing rights have been sold to Murmansk, apparently; in any case, there isn't a single boat on the water. A fairly battered wooden chapel at the end of a little rocky spit. Below, a collapsed landing stage. Further away, the remains of a rustic jetty are poking out of the water, timber cribs filled with stones. The coast path follows the old railway track that used to run from the station to the camp entrance. Sleepers sunk in the sandy soil are still visible, and on the sides, the ballast stones. (It is moving to see the materialisation of things that come from the dual immateriality of the past and of reading: events that occurred a very long time ago, which I know about only through books – this is their concrete trace, here and now.) On alighting, we were greeted with punches and blows from rifle butts, wrote Oleg Volkov in his memoir. There were shacks abandoned by the British Army who came to lend the Whites a helping hand during the civil war. Inside, a decor that hadn't yet become habitual in Russian life: bedsteads, lice, bugs, smells, the violence of the *urkas*. Photograms of the time (because, unlike the other camps, those of the Solovetsky Islands were used in Soviet propaganda) show the arrival of a convoy, men and women carrying suitcases, shopping bags and large bundles, watched by soldiers in caps and high boots, their guns held in front of them.

Alexey Feodosievich was one of those men, one of those poor wretches who went through the entrance over which there was a red star and the inscription *KEMPERPUNKT*, the abbreviation of *Kemsky peresylny punkt*, 'Kem Transit Point'. He arrives on 11 May. He is to stay there for one month. He writes several long letters to his wife (he will write 168 during his years in detention). He is worried about Eleonora, their daughter. 'If I don't manage to have my case reviewed this year,' he says, 'you should give little Elia your surname. It will make things easier for her, but for me she will always be my little Elishka, my little star. Otherwise she'll have problems when she starts kindergarten and later at school. She will live through times even more interesting than ours,' he writes. 'Take care of her and of yourself. You are my life. Strength of mind will help us overcome the pain of separation.' In prison, he adds, he has thought back over his entire life and realises that for thirty-five years he has voluntarily relinquished all the privileges of the class into which he was born. He refused financial support from his father, preferring the poverty of student life. Having a clear conscience vis-à-vis the working class for thirty-five years, and vis-à-vis the Soviet regime for sixteen years, he says, gives him strength and courage.

The camp is not all violence. Or rather, it is in itself pure violence, but within it are spaces, moments, where an educational utopia survives. This is hard to understand in the history of the Solovki camp, of which Kem is the antechamber: in the midst of the most extreme brutality, primarily one that arbitrarily robs thousands of innocents of freedom, brief interstices subsist where the mind can take refuge, like clearings in a dark forest: the library, where Wangenheim will work, is one such place, as are the theatre and the lectures. That is what makes the Solovki camp unique, which also explains why the Soviet propaganda of the 1920s held it up as a shining example. Gorky, for example, paid a visit to the Solovetsky Islands in 1929 (between two stays on the Amalfi coast!). Like Édouard Herriot touring Ukraine, he was only shown edifying sights, and he returned enchanted, and shouted about it, of course, since that was what was expected of him. This uniqueness diminished over the years, but it was still a feature in the mid-1930s. Afterwards, things took a more sinister turn, but then, it was no longer a matter of showcasing what was going on. So Wangenheim gives lectures on 'the conquest of the stratosphere' – about which he knows a thing or two. And he is heartened when passing prisoners greet him respectfully, calling him 'Professor'. Doubtless the hardest thing to bear is the loss of esteem.

One day, on the wireless, he hears an interview with Schmidt, the 'hero of the Arctic', who has just survived the Chelyuskin expedition. 'You can't imagine the state I was in,' he writes to Varvara Ivanovna. 'His expedition was only one component of that Polar Year to which I devoted so much energy and time, and while he receives praise and medals, I can't get anyone to listen to me . . .' He writes to Stalin, to Mikhail Kalinin, but receives no reply. He cannot believe that his letter will remain unanswered. 'On 9 March I wrote to Comrade Stalin that I have not lost and never will lose my faith in the Party. There are moments when my faith wavers, but I fight it and will not allow myself to be crushed.' There are moments when the humiliation of having become a person whose letters receive no reply, the awareness of his absurd helplessness, get the better of him. There are circumstances in which a person acquires true self-knowledge and a knowledge of others. Could not Gorky, he asks, Gorky who celebrated the proud man, Gorky 'our Soviet Voltaire', show concretely that he is capable of fighting for the honour of a Communist?

On 10 June 1934, the ship *Udarnik* ('shock worker'), takes him with a contingent of prisoners to the Solovetsky Islands. After a few hours on the water, white cathedrals appear out of the sea, ridging the horizon. The bulbous bell-towers rise up like hot-air balloons, reflected in the pale glassy water under a bank of motionless clouds, then the outline of the walls of the 'Kremlin', the fortress, emerges between the squat towers with silver-painted wooden roofs, the dark ring of the forest stretching all around it: does he have the heart to surrender himself to this very slow, very beautiful, sight?

Yury Chirkov is fifteen when he is outrageously accused of having planned to blow up bridges and assassinate Stanislav Kosior, the General Secretary of the Communist Party of Ukraine (who gets what is coming to him – he is shot in 1939), and Stalin himself. This is in the midst of the madness following the very real assassination of Sergey Kirov, a leading Party figure in Leningrad and potential rival of Stalin. On 1 September 1935, the adolescent schoolboy Chirkov, sentenced for terrorism, lands on the Solovetsky Islands. He is frail-looking but is exceptionally intelligent, curious and determined, and, what is more, he has what can only be described as an extreme disposition towards happiness (the happiness that Isaac Babel saw as 'a character trait' of the Bolsheviks), whatever the circumstances. There is nothing particularly joyful about those that awaited him, but no matter, he is determined not to miss any opportunity to be enthralled and to learn. The appearance of the monastery wreathed in fog, shimmering in the rising sun as the

Udarnik enters Prosperity Bay at dawn on 1 September causes him to forget for a moment the horror of his situation: still a child, alone, removed from his family, thrown for many long years into the world of the camps (he will not leave until twenty years later, after the death of the man he was alleged to have wanted to assassinate). Some people would throw themselves overboard for less.

But not him. His young age and physical frailty spare him forced labour, tree felling and sawing. He is soon made assistant librarian. Because there is a library in the camp, a large library even – 30,000 books, including several thousand in foreign languages: especially French, German and English. Some of these books have come from the prisoners themselves; either they brought them with them or their families sent them. In the 1920s, the Solovetsky Islands had been the capital of old Russia, of the *byvshie*, the people of the past. They could all have been (were) characters out of Chekhov. People who read, who had books. In the 1930s, the proportion of former aristocrats or intellectuals on the islands diminished, because there were more socialist hostelries to accommodate them, many other establishments were opened, and then above all mass deportations of peasants had begun: that makes a lot of people. But there were still a large number of *byvshie*, and in any case, the books of the former prisoners remained. And then, initially – an almost idealistic period compared with the police age into which the USSR is sinking – the camp administrators themselves sometimes had books brought in. Ultimately, they came from the same sources, the libraries of the enemies of the people, confiscated along with all their possessions, and it sometimes happened that a prisoner found his own bookplate in a volume borrowed from the camp. In short, there is a vast library on the Solovetsky Islands, housed under the roof of the 'Kremlin', the fortress-monastery, and Yury Chirkov is going to work there, side by side, for two years, with the man he respectfully calls 'Professor Wangenheim' and who is in charge of the foreign language books section.

Newly arrived, seeing that he is surrounded by scholars, Yury decides not to let these years be wasted, the camp will be his university, and he sets himself a syllabus worthy of the entrance examination to a top university: mathematics, physics, German (he wants to be able to read Goethe and Schiller), ancient history with Hans Mommsen, Russian history, physical and economic geography . . . to start with (then will come French, economics and the study of the 'Constitutions of bourgeois countries'). And it is Professor Wangenheim who will teach him mathematics and physics. In the fascinating memoir he left of his life in the camps, Yury Chirkov sketched with fine brushstrokes a portrait of the professor: earnest, a little starchy, not much inclined to joking, contrary to what his daughter believes she remembers. He resembled, he said, the portrait of Alexander Herzen by Nikolay Ge – who, with his broad forehead, beard and grey hair, had something of Victor Hugo about him. Yury admires him, but it does not appear that there was ever any familiarity between the two. Chirkov's recollection is slightly mistaken when he gives, among the reasons for the arrest of his mathematics teacher, the *Osoaviakhim* high-altitude balloon disaster, which occurred when Wangenheim had already been in the Lubyanka for three weeks. He mentions another, which was after all quite feasible in the sinisterly preposterous world of Stalinism: at an international scientific congress that he was chairing, contrary to instructions from on high, he allegedly gave an opening speech in French and not in Russian. In any case, he was 'very cultured, and had a perfect command of French and German'. He had a difficult temperament, says Chirkov, and at first had not looked favourably on the arrival of an adolescent, presumed to be disorganised and noisy, in the silent, orderly microcosm of the library. Wangenheim comes across as a man who was not always very generous (he didn't share the provisions his wife sent him), but capable of 'putting on his Sunday best' to go and yell at the camp administrators when they try to prevent Yury from attending the only visit he will ever have from his mother (she will soon die, his father too). He appears not to have lost his Communist faith, despite everything: one day, during an argument, he loses his temper because he will not accept that ranks, abolished after the Revolution, should be reintroduced into the Red Army.

One of Yury's instructors is Pyotr Ivanovich Weigel who teaches him German. He is a Catholic prelate, born in Saratov province, among the Germans of the Volga. He studied in Göttingen then at the Gregorian University in

Rome, going on to become a missionary in Paraguay and the Upper Amazon, on the border between Brazil and Peru: he is a monsignor who has encountered snakes and poisoned arrows. Sent to the USSR by the Vatican to investigate the situation of the Catholics, he was arrested and convicted of an extraordinary number of offences – espionage, sabotage, counter-revolutionary propaganda and even armed insurrection ... In addition to Russian and German, he speaks Italian, Spanish and English, and reads Latin, Greek and Hebrew. A number of remarkable figures meet in the library. Shattered destinies, paths which should never have crossed, bundled together on an island close to the Arctic Circle, by the iron fist of the arbitrary. Some, including Chirkov, will survive and bear witness, others – the majority – will die. Pyotr Ivanovich Weigel is not the only prelate, there is also Shio Batmanishvili, a Georgian bishop who has translated Dante into his language; Pavel Florensky is an Orthodox priest with an encyclopaedic mind, two qualities that do not always go hand in hand. A friend of Andrei Bely, philosopher, mathematician, physicist and chemist, navigating with ease between theology and the theory of relativity ... He has worked with the Bolsheviks in scientific and industrial institutions, which does not save him from being arrested under article 58, paragraph 10 (anti-Soviet and counter-revolutionary propaganda). In the Solovki camp, he runs a small unit, which he set up, to extract iodine from seaweed.

There are monks, musicians including Leonid Privalov, one of the leading Russian baritones, a singer at the Kirov theatre (now the Mariinsky) and at the Baku Opera House, the pianist Nikolay Vygodsky, former teacher at the Moscow conservatoire, Shcherbovich, leader of the Bolshoi orchestra, there is the Romany orchestra conducted by the Romany king in person, Gogo Stanescu still known as Trifolo the Mardulako, also sentenced under a whole raft of paragraphs from article 58 (espionage on behalf of Romania, terrorism, anti-Soviet propaganda, etc.). There is Les Kurbas, a renowned Ukrainian film and theatre director ousted in 1933 from the Berezil (Spring) theatre which he founded in Kiev, charged with avant-gardism cut off from the masses. There are engineers and philosophers, Pavel Ivensen who survives and will later design the Proton rocket, and Mikhail Burkov, a friend to animals, who threw a tripe pie at the black limousine belonging to a Party bigwig that had just run over a little dog, and who will not survive. There are doctors, Professor Oshman from Baku who accidentally smashed a bust of Stalin, Grigory Kotlyarevsky a philologist who became political commissar of the Black Sea Fleet and who runs the library in a relaxed manner until it is 'taken in hand' in January 1937, when he is sacked at the same time as Wangenheim, 'Ukrainian Latinists reciting Virgil', a Japanese 'spy' who acts as the camp barber, an Austrian former officer, an accomplished horseman who axed to death several thugs who were attacking him, a German Communist, Hermann Kupferstein, who was involved in the assassination of the young Nazi party 'martyr' Horst Wessel, and a former Hungarian secretary of the Comintern

Executive Committee now lighthouse keeper of the Solovetsky Islands. There is the last Jagiellon prince, descendant of the grand dukes of Lithuania and the kings of Poland and Hungary. A bald old man, ruddy-faced, shabby, greedy, courteous, who dies of indigestion in his bed one night having managed to scrounge three rations of bread.

It is an assorted little company, cultured and cosmopolitan, that gravitates around the library. On the fringes of the camp, but not at all clandestine, accepted, encouraged even, by the administration for a long time. Alongside the exhausting hard labour, the miserable rations of bread and dishwater coffee, freezing isolator cells and executions, there is also this life, a vestige of bygone days. That is the paradox of the SLON, the 'Solovki Special Purpose Camp'. It's a story that is hard to understand – I do not claim to have grasped it fully, perfectly. In none other of the countless camps of the Gulag is this peculiarity of the Solovetsky Islands to be found. An erudite Catholic bishop rubs shoulders with a former head of the assault sections of the German Communist Party, an austere meteorologist crosses paths with a Romany king. Extreme political violence has thrown them together here, on this island hemmed in by ice six months of the year, enveloped by the long night of winter draped in the aurora borealis. An extreme miscarriage of justice has torn them from their families, their jobs, their homes, from all the big and small things that are the fabric of a person's life and whose memory haunts them; but this violence, this miscarriage of justice permits the possibility of a human existence to endure, for a while at least. There is the theatre, where Les Kurbas performs Ostrovsky or Labiche alongside edifying plays, there are concerts – they play Brahms and Rachmaninoff's Second Piano Concerto declaring it is Tchaikovsky to conceal the fact that they dare play the music of an émigré; for a while there is a 'regional studies society' that takes an interest in the islands' fauna and archaeology. And so there are books from the former libraries of St Petersburg, Kiev and Moscow, deported with their readers, and which are to be more faithful friends than many. Russian classics, naturally, but also foreign, a lot of French in particular – French was still a major language in Russia – Stendhal, Balzac, Victor Hugo . . . In a village library in Yarsevo, some 500 kilometres south of the Solovetsky Islands, I came across Stendhal's *Memoirs of an Egotist* and *The Life of Henry Brulard*, with the same profile portrait as the one on the first complete works, published in 1913 by Édouard and Honoré Champion, and stamped with the words 'OGPU SLON Library' inside a purple triangle. Chirkov remembers having held in his hands an edition of *Les Misérables*, annotated in Russian and French by Turgenev and a first edition of Voltaire's *The Maid of Orleans* . . . during his stay at the Solovki camp he read Élisée Reclus's *Géographie universelle* as happily as Stendhal's *The Charterhouse of Parma* or Henry Fielding's *History of Tom Jones*. And even, in July 1937, the first two volumes of Proust's *In Search of Lost Time*, 'very fashionable then', he says . . . It could sometimes happen that relatively recent books – *Within a Budding Grove* had been published in 1919 – reached the Solovetsky Islands. A young man discovering Marcel, Albertine and Andrée's intermittences of the heart in a Soviet prison camp! Imagining the beach at Balbec or Rivebelle restaurant bang in the middle of the White Sea: unlikely as it may be, this situation occurred . . .

II

My faith in the Soviet authorities has in no way been shaken, writes Alexey Feodosievich in his letter of 18 June 1934, just after his arrival at Solovki. Nevertheless it is curious that there has been no response to my appeals over the past five months. He has written to Kalinin and to Stalin several times. Kalinin is nothing but a figurehead, it is a done deal, an accommodating old Bolshevik – so accommodating that in 1938 he will allow his wife to be sent to the Gulag without protest – but all the same he is president of the presidium of the Supreme Soviet, he could do something. I have been designated to do agricultural work in the greenhouses, he continues. The day's work begins at six o'clock in the morning and ends at four o'clock in the afternoon – that's ten hours without stopping, without a break. The work isn't too hard, however, his situation is very 'privileged' compared to the vast mass of prisoners whose labours consist of felling trees and floating logs, because he has been acknowledged as suffering from a nervous disease, he has anxiety attacks when he is alone in a room or when he looks at the sky from an open space, which is the last straw for a meteorologist. I gave a talk on the conquest of the Arctic, he writes. Nature is beautiful, but the sun gives very little warmth. Has Comrade Stalin received my letter?

My faith in the Soviet authorities has not been shaken. His handwriting is tiny, cramped, hard to decipher, on the pages of school exercise books sent to him by his wife, Varvara. The foot of pages three and four is reserved for drawings or pressed flowers for his daughter, so that Varvara can fold the sheet and cut off the bottom to give to Eleonora. She has told her that her father has gone off to the far north on a long voyage of discovery. I live in a cell with five other people, he writes to Varvara, we get along well. I have been identified as belonging to the third health category (there are four, excluding the disabled), my work isn't hard, and when I have some free time I make mosaics with stone chippings. He soon becomes extremely adept at this technique, which he uses to unexpected ends: he makes portraits of Stalin. Does he do this out of conviction, or to pull the wool over the eyes of the camp administrators and thus obtain a visiting permit for Varvara? So that Comrade Stalin will hear about it and answer his letters, and finally dispense justice? In any case, blinkeredness or pathetic cunning, there is something sinister about seeing this man, this scholar, making of his own volition the portrait of the man in whose name he is being crucified. I have been given permission to send Elia something I have made for her, he writes, a little box decorated with stones from Popov Island, crushed brick and coal. I read little, but I intend to make an effort soon.

Ivan Akulov, Procurator General of the USSR, visits the camp, and drops in to see this prisoner who has the effrontery to be discontented with his conviction and to bombard the highest authorities, even up to the Supreme Comrade, with protestations of his innocence. (Well, for the time being, this Akulov in his tightly belted leather coat is Procurator General of the USSR, but what he does not know – what neither of them knows – is that he will be shot three days before the miserable wretch in front of him babbling his complaints in a choked voice.) I am not pleased with myself, Alexey Feodosievich tells his wife, I was afraid I'd have a screaming fit. I had taken some drops of valerian. I forgot to say important things, the slightest question made me lose my train of thought. Akulov came into my cell without warning, with a group of officials. I'd just finished a portrait of Stalin with different-coloured stones, it was standing on the table. I felt very uncomfortable because they might have thought I'd put it there on purpose. Anyway, I hope he grasped the full horror of my situation. (One can't help thinking that to avoid putting himself in such situations, it would have been best not to make the portrait of the man whose fingers Osip Mandelstam, writing at the same time, compared to worms and his moustache to cockroaches.)

There are five of us in the cell, he writes, hard-working people, a young man I'd like to help become educated. We're a bit cramped, but with five it's easier to guard the cell, there's always someone at home. I still haven't had a reply from Kalinin or from Stalin or from the Central Control Commission of the Central Committee. I don't know what to think. I can't believe that no one cares about the truth. I have enough respect for the Party and for the Soviet leaders to carry on hoping that sooner or later the truth will prevail, and this belief gives me great strength. He cannot believe, he tries hard not to believe, he probably senses that he is beginning to doubt; seven months have already gone by since his arrest, it is July 1934, but he knows that if he allows doubt to creep in, he will lose all hope.

We're in July, it's very hot, he writes, an almost southern heat. The sea sparkles in front of the ancient fortress, offering a dream of freedom. From eight o'clock in the morning until ten or eleven o'clock at night, sometimes midnight, I work planting trees around the 'Kremlin', but the work isn't too tiring and it distracts me from my thoughts. No news of my appeals to Stalin and Kalinin. I don't know what to think. Deep down I fear that no one cares about the truth. I can't help being assailed by terrible doubts. For the time being, I am fighting them, but it's difficult. I work hard, intellectually I do nothing, but in time I'll buckle down. In time . . . He is beginning to understand that there is a possibility that he will be there for a long time. I live with people who are very different from me, he writes. Recently,

while washing the floor, I had a dizzy spell and the Ukrainian (who allocates the chores) let me off finishing the job.
Have you been to see Gorky? Here, they speak ill of him,
they remember his visit. The visit mentioned by Alexey
Feodosievich is that of June 1929, when Gorky visited *en
famille*, with his son and daughter-in-law all dressed in black
leather, and returned very satisfied with his excursion. A
few months later, mass executions took place at Solovki.
Understandably, the 'Soviet Voltaire' had not made a very
good impression on the deportees. Since then, he has done
a lot more for Gulag tourism: in August 1933, he took 120
writers on a cruise along the White Sea–Baltic Canal whose
construction, just completed, had cost the lives of several
tens of thousands of *zeks*, drawn chiefly from the Solovetsky
Islands. One hundred and twenty gentlemen in white suits
questioning the slaves at the locks: you happy, my good
man? You rehabilitated through work? The trip resulted in
a book that had just been published in 1934: *The Stalin
White Sea–Baltic Canal*. Meanwhile, in France, Louis
Aragon enthused about 'the extraordinary experience' of
rehabilitation through work. As for Gorky . . . Like Schmidt,
he had other fish to fry.

Deep down I fear that no one cares about the truth. I'm
working in the 'Kremlin' gardens, writes Alexey Feodosievich on 20 July, and here we really feel a little ashamed
for him. We wish he could be more articulate, more rebellious, but no, he continues to be a good Communist, a good
Soviet crammed with ideology, his convictions seemingly

unshaken by the fate that awaits him and which he is not the only one to suffer. Each flower bed, he says, tells a different story for the edification of the viewer. Combining stones and flowers, he makes a bed with the red star, another with the slogan 'Work is a matter of Honour', echoing another, inscribed over the entrance of the Nazi camps. He works on the portraits of Lenin and Dzerzhinsky . . . Yes, even Felix Dzerzhinsky, the founder of the Cheka! There were rebels, such as the extraordinary Yevgeniya Yaroslavskaya-Markon, who, disabled as a result of an accident, nonetheless attempted to help her husband escape, failed, was in turn deported to the Solovetsky Islands, refused to obey in any way, and one day wore a sign around her neck on which she had written 'Death to the Chekists!', and ended up being shot in 1931, not without having spat in the face of the camp commander. But Alexey Feodosievich is not a rebel. It is not in his nature or in his upbringing. His favourite clouds are not the ones that herald a storm. And he makes a portrait of the founder of the Cheka . . . And writing his story eighty years later, I find myself loath to mention this pathetic trait, but why? I would rather he were uncompromising, like Yevgeniya, I would rather admire him, but he was not admirable and that is perhaps what is interesting. He's an average sort, a Communist who asks no questions, or rather who is now forced to start asking some, but it is only after suffering an extraordinary assault that he hesitantly reaches this point. He is an ordinary innocent. Dreyfus too was disappointing, apparently, in another way.

ARITHMETIC

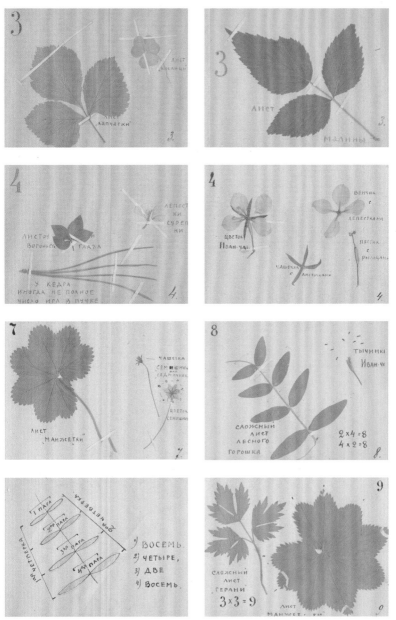

'One of my acquaintances made a leaf collection to teach his daughter to count:
1, then 2, then 3, then 4 leaves …' (Pavel Florensky, letter of 3 July 1935)

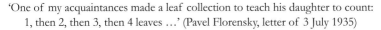

ARITHMETIC

GEOMETRY

Pentagon, square, circle, ellipse, spiral, triangle, symmetry, asymmetry.

GEOMETRY

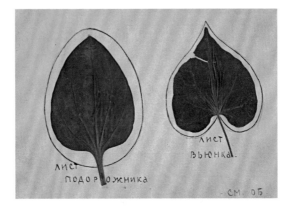

ЛИСТ
ПОДОРОЖНИКА

ЛИСТ
ВЬЮНКА.

СМ. ОБ.

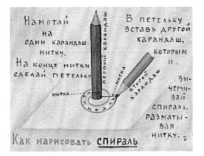

Намотай на один карандаш нитку. На конце нитки сделай петельку.

первый карандаш

нитка

второй карандаш

В петельку, вставь другой карандаш, которым и вычерчивай спираль, разматывая нитку.

Как нарисовать **СПИРАЛЬ**

Обрежь катушку.

Сделай дырочку.

Возьми ниточку, сделай узелок. Продерни ниточку через дырочку так, чтобы узелок был внутри. На другом конце ниточки сделай петельку. Вставь в неё карандаш. Оберни нитку около катушки. Держи катушку крепко. Веди карандаш натягивая нитку, — получишь **СПИРАЛЬ**

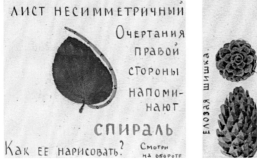

ЛИСТ НЕСИММЕТРИЧНЫЙ

Очертания правой стороны напоминают **СПИРАЛЬ**

Как её нарисовать? Смотри на обороте

ЕЛОВАЯ ШИШКА

СВЕРХУ

чешуйка

С БОКУ

СПИРАЛЬ

Сверху чешуйки кажутся расположенными по СПИРАЛИ.

GEOMETRY

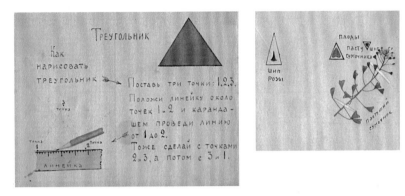

ТРЕУГОЛЬНИК

Как нарисовать треугольник →

Поставь три точки: 1, 2, 3.
Положи линейку около точек 1 и 2 и карандашем проведи линию от 1 до 2.
Тоже сделай с точками 2 и 3, а потом с 3 и 1.

точка
точка 1   точка 2
ЛИНЕЙКА

ШИП
РОЗЫ

ПЛОДЫ
ПАСТУШЬЕЙ
СУМОЧНИКА

ПАСТУШЬЙ
СУМОЧНИК

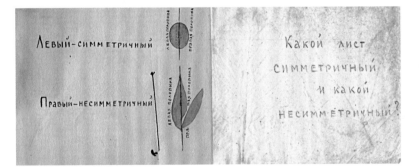

Левый – симметричный

Правый – несимметричный

левая половина   правая половина
левая половина   правая половина

Какой лист
симметричный
и какой
несимметричный?

ЛЕВЫЙ ЛИСТ
состоит
из
ДВУХ ПОХОЖИХ –
– симметричных
ПОЛОВИНОК

ЛИСТ
СИМ
МЕТРИЧНЫЙ

ПРАВЫЙ ЛИСТ
состоит
из
ДВУХ РАЗЛИЧНЫХ
– несимметричных
ПОЛОВИНОК

ЛИСТ
НЕ-
СИМ-
МЕ-
ТРИЧНЫЙ

Какой
лист
СИММЕТРИЧНЫЙ
и
КАКОЙ
НЕСИММЕТРИЧНЫЙ?

BERRIES

'I'm sending her the drawing of a berry that's found here, I'm planning to make a collection of flowers and berries for her.'
(Letter of 20 July 1935)

ANIMALS

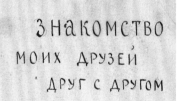

'Meet my friends.'

'It may seem strange, but this playful little grey creature comforts me.' (Letter of 20 September 1935)

'I found the time to draw a reindeer for Elia.' (Letter of 17 December 1936)

RIDDLES

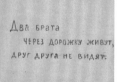

'Two brothers live beside a path/ but never see one another'

'Seventy coats/ but no buttons'

'With no door and no windows/ A house full of people'

'Sitting in the spoon/ legs dangling'

'Near a hole/ white doves'

RIDDLES

‘Mother and daughter/ Mother and daughter/ Grandmother and grand-daughter/How many are they in total?’

‘A girl in prison/ Her plait outside’

‘Steel nose/Cotton tail’

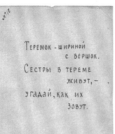

‘A house a few centimetres in size/ Sisters live in it/Guess what they’re called’

RIDDLES

"ПЕЛЕНКИ" У КРАСНОГО КЛЕВЕРА

КЛЕВЕР. Когда родится ребенок, его защищают от холода, ветра пеленками, рубашечками и одеяльцем. Оказывается, "пеленки" и "рубашечки" встречаются и у растений. Они служат для защиты от непогоды, называются только иначе. Вот у клевера молодые побеги, пока они еще боятся непогоды, спрятаны в широкие прилистники, которые совершенно окутывают побег. Пока он молод — (см №1.) На №2 этот прилистник отделен, чтобы его легче было рассмотреть, а на №3 он для этого даже отогнут.

Но вот молодой побег понемногу растет и вылезает из прилистника. Оказывается, что, вылезая из первой "пеленки"-прилистника, он защищен еще и второй — см №4, №5. Если этот побег несет наверху цветок, то у этого цветка еще особая "пеленка", как это видно на №6. Цветок клевера — сложный цветок, он состоит из многих маленьких цветочков. И каждый цветок защищен в свою очередь четвертой "пеленкой" — зеленой чашечкой. Чашечка со всех сторон закрывает еще совсем молодой цветок — см бутон на №7, и защищает только низ цветка, когда он распустится — см. №8.

'The red clover's swaddling'

Холодно котику. Он свернулся клубочком. Как будто стремится подставить холоду возможно меньшую поверхность своего тела, чтобы оно меньше охлаждалось. Лежит он клубочком и греет-ся. Стало тепло.

КЛЕВЕР НА НОЧЬ СВЕРТЫВАЕТСЯ

У клевера — тройной лист. Днем, когда тепло, этот лист совершенно развернут. Вся поверхность его открыта солнцу и воздуху. Но вот при-

'The red clover snuggles up for the night'

PLANTS AND THE CLIMATE

Шуба у растений

Как и у серебристого тополя, у некоторых растений шубой покрываются только молодые части.

Так у ивы (см. №1-4) молодые листья покрыты лесом волосков с обеих сторон, тогда как у старых листьев остаётся слабое опушение только на нижней стороне.

Сравни два листа герани (см. №5): один молодой внизу, только что вылезающий из пазухи взрослого листа, кажется серым, так как покрыт густым слоем волосков, другой – взрослый лист – без опушения. Подобное и у клевера. Головка бутонов, где спрятаны ещё молодые, нежные цветки (см. №6), – защищена лесом усиков, покрытых волосками, тогда как у головки со взрослыми цветами (см. №7) этого леса усиков уже не видно.

Шуба у растений

Шуба греет человека. А почему? Потому, что среди волосинок меха много воздуха, а воздух не пропускает ни холода ни тепла.

У некоторых растений тоже шуба из тончайших волосиков.

Что происходит в шубе, когда дует сильный ветер? Волоски шубы не пропускают ветра, среди них тихо.

Этим пользуются растения. Зайди в лес во время ветра.

Кругом шумит, верхушки деревьев качаются, а среди деревьев внизу тихо. А если нет ветра, то и вода испаряется, высыхает медленно.

Вот для того, чтобы защищаться от холода и от сильного высыхания, у некоторых растений на листьях, стеблях, чашечках находится целый густой лес волосиков, который составляет их шубу.

Посмотри на листья на обороте. Снизу они сизые — это от того что снизу они покрыты шубой из волосков. А у серебристого тополя молодые листочки с обеих сторон покрыты шубкой, которая бережёт их от холода

'Plants' fur-trimmed coats'

White clover, willow, silver poplar, red clover …

NATURAL PHENOMENA

'I gave ten lectures on the aurora borealis. I have seen several, mostly they are in the form of an arc, but once I saw curtains of green rays shimmering in the sky and undulating as if in the wind.'

(Letter of 22 March 1936)

'Did you receive the bullfinch and *varakusha* nests?'
(Final letter, of 19 September 1937)

LETTERS

Дорогая моя
звездочка Элечка!
Наконец-то и к нам при-
ходит весна. Правда, нет
настоящего южного и да-
же московского тепла, но
деревья уже распускаются,
я уже варил себе моло-
дую крапиву, прилетели кри-
кливые чайки. Может быть

РЯБИНА

Дорогая моя звездочка Элечка!
Ты напи-
сала мне,
что не по-
лучила
черно-сере-
бристой
лисы. Посылаю вторично ее портрет.
Она свободно бегает, не боится людей и

'Did you get your second Arctic fox?'
(Final letter, of 19 September 1937)

'Because he was unjustly convicted,' Bernard Lazare wrote of him (cited by Charles Péguy), 'everybody expected the most heroic virtues of Dreyfus. He was innocent, that was already a great deal.'

I have been chosen as a shock worker, he writes, that's why in July I was allowed to send you four letters, it's a very effective spur. He has one day's rest, which he spends picking mushrooms and blueberries. He finishes the portrait of Stalin in stone chippings and is pleased with it. He is in the hospital, they treat his hand with the 'blue light' of ultraviolet rays, but the doctor is sceptical. He is authorised to take a daily shower, and thinks this treatment will soothe his nerves. He is also permitted to send a broken pince-nez to the mainland to be repaired. Authorisation is required for everything, as if he were a child. He tries to read a little. Using stone chippings, he depicts a black-and-white bullock against a background of meadows and sky: that is better than making Stalin's portrait, but is there not something insolent about doing the portrait of a bullock after that of the Supreme Comrade? This thought does not seem to have crossed his mind, it doesn't look bad, he says (of the bullock). He wonders whether it has been pointless urging Varvara to go and see Gorky, who is so unpopular in the camp, seemingly with good reason. And Dimitrov, has she tried to see him? Perhaps the fact that he himself had been unjustly accused will make him sympathetic towards Wangenheim's situation? What about Schmidt, has she asked him? Perhaps his fame won't stop him from fighting for the truth? He refuses to believe that people, these people, these comrades, have become blind and do not want to regain their sight.

I don't remember if I told you that Stalin received my petition, he writes in September. Akulov told me. It's four months since I sent it, eight months that I've been here, and I'm still wondering why. The days of the midnight sun are over, the sky is more and more autumnal, soon it will be the equinox. We hardly see any more seagulls. The seagulls leave the islands as winter approaches, before the sea freezes over, and they come back in late spring. I'm planning to send you a parcel, he adds, I'll put in it a writing case decorated with a mosaic, and my broken pince-nez. My condition has worsened, perhaps with the arrival of autumn. I received your parcel, in the hospital where I am forced to remain. The hospital, according to Yury Chirkov who was briefly an orderly and then a nurse, is not at all one of those places where prisoners went to die that were seen in other camps. Top-level prisoner doctors work there and the director, a renowned Moscow paediatrician, ensures the place is kept scrupulously clean. Physically, I'm fine, he writes, it's my nerves that need treating. I am involved in organising the library and the reading room, but rather by correspondence.

The days of the midnight sun are over, the sky is more and more autumnal. During the white nights, the sun skims the horizon in the north-west then rises, the sky is golden in the gaps between the clouds, the treetops permanently lit up. In this light, the world looks like the sort of place you see in dreams. Autumn comes quickly, he writes, the polar night will soon be here. Today we lit the stoves for the first time. The forest is yellow and ochre, the trees are losing their leaves. I don't know what I'll do when I come out of hospital, I don't want to work outdoors, because although I love nature, my age and my fragile nerves make me fear the cold. My comrades send me newspapers, he writes, but I can't read them. Even the simplest things irritate me. Reading Litvinov's speech to the League of Nations I had to start over again three times. I avoid reading things about the Arctic. The weather's turning nasty, the days are getting much shorter, there's very little light in the evening. Cold autumn rains are falling and on 2 October it snowed. The snow settled for two days. I'm busy sorting out the library classification system, I write lessons. Did you enquire about my second petition to the Central Control Commission? he writes on 6 October. I sent it on 6 August. Have you been to see Schmidt? I'd like to receive your replies before shipping comes to a halt. I can't help being assailed by terrible doubts.

The days are growing rapidly shorter. According to my calculations, he writes at the end of October, you haven't received letters sixteen and nineteen (the prisoners number their letters so as to keep track of which ones arrive and which ones get lost). Yours arrive very erratically. I study Capablanca chess, but I can't play because it's bad for my nerves. You ask how to get to the Solovetsky Islands, but unfortunately that's impossible. To receive visits, the prisoners are transferred to the mainland for a few days, but I don't have authorisation, he writes. These desperately longed-for visits are also a huge blow to the morale of the deportees who relive with their loved ones the poignant memory of their past life. Chirkov describes his overwhelming sadness after he met his mother in Kem (the time when Professor Wangenheim interceded on his behalf with the camp administrators), and he had the (justified) premonition that he would never see her again. Perhaps I've allowed life to get the better of me, writes Alexey Feodosievich on the last day of October. I didn't see the new moral code developing and I don't understand what's going on at all. I've been refused visiting rights a second time, he adds.

Then comes the October Revolution anniversary holiday (in November of our calendar). This is the first time he is spending it in these conditions, he says. He comes out of hospital, his morale very low. He decorates the library, he hand-writes slogans. His cellmates went to a theatre performance, but he didn't want to join them. I find it painful to go without you, he writes to Varvara. He prefers to remain alone guarding the cell. The last time he went to the theatre . . . or rather he didn't go . . . They were supposed to go to the Bolshoi together, he recalls, the night of his arrest. In two days, he calculates, it will be the end of the tenth month of this nightmare. How bitter he is at the thought of those ten wasted months while the country so badly needed experts! He notices that his name has been removed as publisher of the translations of the Swedish meteorologist Tor Bergeron. That is upsetting, but a trifle compared to the rest. I can't draw the way I used to, he says, I have less time and there's not enough daylight. On the days when there's no sunshine, the cell is very dark. Yesterday I started to draw a flower for Elishka, but couldn't finish it because it was too dark. Awake or asleep, he says, there is no rest for the soul.

In two days, it will be the end of the tenth month of this nightmare. He has his new posting, to the library, which isn't too tiring for him, he comments. He gave a lecture on the stratosphere, somewhat sad because he recollected the time when he spoke on the subject with Prokofyev, the pilot of the *USSR-1* high-altitude balloon. The memories of those golden days came back to him, it was just over a year ago. Lying on his bench, he pictured himself driving through a ghost Moscow at night, the city barely visible in the fog that the car headlamps had difficulty penetrating, the stars on the Kremlin's towers glimpsed amid swirls of red vapour like that of a fire, as if Moscow were burning for the second time. That fog was a bad omen, and on the Kuntsevo airfield, the vast envelope sparkling with millions of pearls of dew in the dawn . . . and then the night of the real departure, which he had spent fine-tuning Molchanov's equipment, anxious about this unforeseen responsibility that had fallen to him, but secretly pleased, too, perhaps, that the lateness of the Leningrad train left him alone at the controls . . . He was the person who had analysed the scientific readings from the flight, in an issue of *Pravda*.

Molchanov, what's become of him? The horror of his situation is not just being separated from his family, it is not just being denigrated, dishonoured and treated as a criminal (and to have colluded in that through his own weakness), it is also no longer to be of any use, no longer to experience the fever, the anxiety and the pride that were his then. How galling it is to think of those wasted months, he writes . . . How galling it is to think that others are carrying on, while I have become this utterly useless person who gives lectures to prisoners, and who will be consigned to oblivion on this island hemmed in by ice and darkness.

I have found something to occupy my spare time during the winter, he writes: working on the meteorological treatise I plan to write, and reading in foreign languages. I've begun *Uncle Tom's Cabin* in French. I'm so busy that I haven't played chess once. The weather is typical of the Solovetsky Islands: it snows for two days, then it all melts, and then comes freezing rain and fog. How are Schmidt and Prokofyev? This Prokofyev is to meet a tragic and eminently romantic end. The son of a peasant, a worker from the age of fifteen, soldier in the Red Army who became an expert on altitude balloons, he invented a complicated launch system which never really worked, usually ending in the fatal twisting of the suspension cables, the accidental opening of a valve and the plummeting of the balloon. After a first crash that had already caused considerable damage, *USSR-3* lifted off again in March 1939, with Prokofyev in command. He could have parachuted out but remained on board.

Severely wounded, as were his two crew, doubtless aware that his decidedly half-baked invention had already caused enough crushed vertebra and gut-wrenching (and even the death of the pilot of the prototype), he put a bullet through his brain in the hospital, while still dreaming of new altitude records. He'd had his hour of glory on 30 September 1933, suspended at 19,000 metres in the deep blue sky, but had never repeated it. If you can, writes Alexey Feodosievich to his wife, send me an English–Russian dictionary. From eight o'clock in the morning until four o'clock in the afternoon, then from five until ten or eleven, I look after the books. The rest of the time I spend eating and sleeping. I find it hard to read. I snatch moments to practise foreign languages. This afternoon I did a drawing for my little girl. I would so love to have spent a year on an Arctic weather station, but willingly, and knowing that I was doing a useful job!

Winter reigns, he writes at the end of November, there are fierce winds, everything is white, the lake's iced over, the sea isn't yet, but it will freeze soon and then we'll be cut off from everything until May. All my thoughts and desires go out towards you, towards you and the Party which must re-establish the truth. I am not losing faith, I don't want to lose it. I'm carrying out the inventory of the library. I have little time to read. I have to put off darning my socks to the end of the week, but every day I find a few minutes to do something for my little girl. I have made myself a big writing desk out of plywood on which I can arrange ink, Indian ink, pencils, brushes, spectacles and pince-nez. Still no news from Akulov, he writes, and apparently there won't be any. My brain refuses to comprehend, all this is such a far cry from my ideas of Bolshevism . . . but I haven't lost faith in the Party. Still that 'faith in the Party' to which he desperately clings to stop himself from going to pieces completely. His insistence that he has held on to it suggests that it was probably deserting him.

All my thoughts go out to you, he writes. I managed to see the Commander of the 13th sector of the BBK a few minutes before he left, and I gave him a letter for Comrade Stalin. He promised me he'd send it immediately and let me know the date it is posted. I beg you, find out from the secretariat whether he has received my petition: this isn't primarily a matter of my personal fate, it is important for the Party above all. I gave a lecture on the possibility of a flight to the moon or Mars with a jet engine, he writes, there were only around thirty people in the audience, but there were a lot of questions. There are only around thirty people who are all dreaming of an unlikely return journey to Moscow or Leningrad or Kiev, to their families, their jobs, the lives they have left behind, but who despite that show an interest in a voyage to the moon . . . 'Numberless are the world's wonders, but none more wonderful than man,' said Sophocles. The sea is battling against the winter, it is frozen but not yet so solidly that shipping must stop. Boats arrive, but fairly infrequently.

A voyage to the moon or Mars. A letter addressed to Comrade Stalin. Comrade Stalin's world is further removed from the deportee Wangenheim than the moon or Mars. On 1 January 1935, he finishes a reverse glass portrait of Comrade Kirov, who was assassinated one month earlier in Leningrad. It is a popular item, this is the fourth one he's been commissioned to do. That evening he plans to give a lecture on a subject he finds fairly original: 'Overview of humanity's conquests in the field of knowledge from the dawn of creation until the construction of socialism and the advent of the classless society'. A theme that is certainly not lacking in ambition. I don't know how it will go down, he says. You refrain from mentioning your material situation, he writes to Varvara, or do the letters in which you talk about it disappear? In any case, the lack of news makes me anxious. For the past three days it's been very cold, but don't worry, we light the stove once a week, it's always warm. The library is heated and we work in good conditions, with the electric light on all the time because the days are very short. I had to move to a new cell, at the moment there are four of us living in fairly cramped conditions, but peacefully. We have to work hard, and I haven't had the time to draw anything for my little star.

For the past three days it's been very cold. The aeroplane brought the newspapers for the library, he writes, I stayed up till four o'clock in the morning filing the first batch, and the following night I was up classifying the second one until seven o'clock in the morning. Then there were the preparations for the Lenin Days. Today I finished at three o'clock in the morning. I did a reverse glass Indian ink portrait of V. M. (most likely Molotov) surrounded by red flags and projects contributing to the construction of socialism: the Dneprostroy [dam], chemicals factories, etc. There's a snowstorm, and violent winds are sweeping the island. Yes, this year is wasted, he writes. If I aggravated someone in Moscow, they could have sent me to run a kolkhoz in the provinces, I have experience of farm work, or I could have spent this year on an Arctic weather station – now that would have made sense – whereas everything that's happening now is utterly absurd. Don't go thinking that my insistence on learning the fate of my petitions to Stalin is because of my naivety, he writes. If Otto Yulyevich knew what was in them, he would consider it his sacred duty as a Communist to do something. Otto Yulyevich is Schmidt, the leader of the *Chelyuskin* expedition. My state of mind is deteriorating. Receiving news of you is the only thing that can cheer me up. You, back home, are living through a unique period in history, each day brings new successes, new triumphs . . . the Seventeenth Congress, the opening of the Metro, how all these events would have thrilled me! You're wrong to think I'm not eating properly. I'm not hungry and I'm even eating too much. My cooking is improving, I've already made a sort of batter pudding for myself and my cellmates, not bad at all.

You're spending a lot of money on the parcels, darling. History cannot justify your suffering. If Stalin knew everything . . . I find it hard to reconcile Bolshevism and utter absurdity in my mind. I broke away from my original class thirty-five years ago, I've given all my strength and knowledge to the working class. I am battling to remain strong, I don't want to lose faith in the Party and the Soviet authorities. I still hope that reason will prevail, that is much more important than my personal fate. You should ask Akulov for a visiting permit, perhaps you'll receive it for when shipping resumes. I'm going to write to Stalin and Voroshilov again. Will it achieve anything? I don't know, but it's my duty before the Party and the country. You write that you want to apply to the Amnesty Commission. But, dearest, only the guilty can be pardoned, and I cannot admit to a non-existent culpability.

I sent my seventh petition to Stalin, he writes, but for the time being I'm getting nowhere and I am at an utter loss to understand. I'm battling to keep my resolve. Don't forget to telephone Otto Yulyevich, I asked him to tell you the outcome of my appeal. We don't know what the hero of the Arctic replied to Varvara, we do not have her letters, but it is easy to guess on reading one of Alexey Feodosievich's subsequent letters: after what happened with Otto Yulyevich, he writes, after his declarations, it is all too clear that the time of truth has not yet come. Schmidt's betrayal is a terrible blow to the illusions he is trying to uphold. For a year he has been struggling against doubt, he knows he must not allow it to grow, that it is like a fire in dry grass, that he must stamp on it before it consumes everything. Suddenly he feels full of ash. It is spring 1935, April. A sinister spring. I have no doubt that History will restore my good name, he writes, but until not long ago I thought that, as soon as my petition arrived, the Party would understand. Apparently that is not the case.

He is at an utter loss to understand. It's spring at the moment, he writes on 18 May, they say a boat might arrive any day now. Only the port is ice-bound. The fields are still covered in snow, the lake's frozen over, but the seagulls are back, and several are already sitting on their nests. Today, he writes, I heard about the *Maxim Gorky* disaster on the radio, and about the huge number of casualties. The brainchild of the engineer Andrey Tupolev (who will soon be sent to the camps), the *Maxim Gorky* was the biggest aeroplane in the world, with a 63-metre wingspan and eight engines, and a panoramic lounge at the front. The flying machine was designed for agitprop, with photography and radio studios, a powerful tannoy system, a printing works and a cinema auditorium, and luminous messages could supposedly be displayed under the wings. The enormous contraption astounded the crowds, until the day in May 1935 when a little biplane looping the loop around it to spice up the air show even more collided with the wing, causing the flying whale to plummet, killing all forty-five passengers and crew. In the Novodevichy cemetery in Moscow, not far from Chekhov's tomb, is a rather spectacular memorial to the dead of the *Maxim Gorky*. Was Arkhangelsky's brother among the passengers? fretted Alexey Feodosievich. Arkhangelsky, a great gynaecologist, was one of the three friends who had not deserted Varvara and Eleonora, along with two meteorologists, Suvorov and Khromov, the same who had 'forgotten' to mention Lenin and Stalin in his article on the 'new ideas' in meteorology. An obstinate Menshevik, for sure . . .

Spring is here now, he writes on 24 May. Nearly all the snow has melted, shipping has begun, the lake is still covered in dirty ice, with gaping black and green holes appearing. And then on 1 June, a massive snowstorm. I didn't go out, he says, it's warm in our room, but I feel this cold in my soul. Have you asked for permission to visit me? Akulov would have given it, but now I don't know any more. Because Akulov has just been replaced by Andrey Vyshinsky, the future state prosecutor of the 'Moscow show trials', the man who demanded that the defendants, Bukharin and other old Bolsheviks, should be executed: 'Shoot these rabid dogs', 'crush the accursed reptiles'. 'The graves of these hateful traitors will grow over with weeds and thistles,' he will declaim. We cannot expect anything of such a man, even if he hasn't yet shown his true colours. My soul seethes with great indignation, writes Alexey Feodosievich. What right do they have to inflict this suffering on an honest servant of the state? I've been here for a year, these past twelve months are a year out of my life. Reading the journals, I come across references to the continuation of my work. We have had little opportunity to talk about it together, you are probably unaware of what I've done, time will pass and all that filled my work life will be forgotten. I have decided to write a report on what I have accomplished so that you and my daughter will know that I wasn't a slacker.

It is just at this point, 10 June 1935, that he mentions the wind and sun registers, as well as wind and solar power which he sees as the reservoirs of the future. He understands that life is going on without him, that his work is continuing without him, that others are picking up his ideas, his work and his dreams, and this is a new torment. He seems to be losing hope of ever returning to that active world where people plan, decide and accomplish, where there is a future, which people claim can be tamed like a wild horse, where, in constructing socialism, they are constructing themselves. Here, on the islands, no future, nothing can be accomplished. This island is the island of the dead. He wants to leave his wife and daughter a testament, so that they at least will not forget that he has not always been a thing, a number in the registers of the NKVD. In 1934, he writes, I should have finished the first atlas of wind energy distribution in the USSR. It will certainly be published, but without me. The same goes for the sun register. Wind power is inexhaustible and renewable. Soon the vast territories of the USSR will be electrified by wind power, and my name will disappear without trace. Solar energy is even more powerful. The future belongs to solar and wind power.

I continue to feel this cold in my soul. We have gone from winter to summer, with very hot days, he writes at the end of June. Thousands of wild geese fly overhead, making their way northwards. He complains that his research on the influence of the weather on the human organism is not progressing. He has always been exercised by this question, he says, which can lead to prolonged life expectancy. In 1932, he organised the first conference in the USSR, and perhaps in the world, on the influence of the climate on humans, he boasts, with doctors, architects, engineers, tree growers and urban planners . . . the purpose was to reflect on the relations between the hydro-meteorological regime and health, the design of apartment buildings, town planning. To think about the habitat and cities in relation to the climate was not so common in those days; he is certainly a pioneer. He reads an article in one newspaper about a new flight to the stratosphere (it must be the *USSR-1 Bis*, in June, which again nearly ended up in a fatal plunge). Once more he sees the fog over Moscow, illuminated by the headlights of Misha the driver, the night spent finetuning the instruments, charting the landing site on the map (and he had calculated it precisely!), the agonising wait for radio messages from the gondola, Prokofyev's nasal voice sending his Communist greetings from high in the sky where he had seen no more of God than Yuri Gagarin would twenty-eight years later, and then the most important part – collating and analysing the readings. On 8 January, that fateful 8 January 1934, he had prepared the report on the results in order to print it for the Seventeenth Congress. It was in his pocket when he was arrested. All he needed to do was proofread his two articles and send the entire thing to the typesetters. You know what happened afterwards, he writes to Varvara. The report was published, but of course without my articles and under a different name.

Recently, he writes in July, I've been lagging a bit behind in my own work because in addition to my regular work in the library I've had to clean the place, the reading room and the toilets. It's a big area and that has taken up all my free time. So I haven't had a moment to draw a riddle for my little girl. I'm sending her the drawing of a berry that's found here, I'm planning to make a collection of flowers and berries for her. As the months go by, he draws apricots, cranberries, a bunch of grapes, cherries, a wild strawberry, gooseberries, raspberries, greengages, blueberries, blackcurrants and redcurrants, plums, a whole fruit salad, and another two which I am not able to identify. He draws a whole series of mushrooms. The riddles are in doggerel, for which I shan't attempt to find an equivalent: 'With no door and no windows / A house full of people' (a bean pod), 'Two brothers live beside a path / but never see one another' (the eyes), with a variant, 'Two brothers see one another without ever meeting / One is trampled on, the other is smoked' (floor and ceiling), or these two, which I quite like: 'Steel nose / cotton tail' (a needle), and 'Seventy coats / but no buttons and no buckles' (a cabbage).

We knew nothing of the north, he writes, even though the polar air masses govern our climate. There was no weather station network in the north, I built it, despite extreme difficulties, including in the vast Siberian wastes. Of course they'll keep quiet about the debt owed to me, all the glory will go to Otto Yulyevich and others, but History will remember. All thanks to my leadership. The results are visible, from Spitzbergen to Uelen in Chukotka. Condemned, forgotten, betrayed, humiliated, he is prone to outbursts of pride, taking credit for everything. When the pilot Sigismund Levanevsky, a handsome fellow known as 'the Russian Lindbergh', is planning a transpolar flight, he writes that if he hadn't battled for three years to set up a network of polar stations, the flight wouldn't be possible (incidentally it was a failure and it was Valery Chkalov who, two years later, flew non-stop from Moscow to Vancouver via the North Pole). The readings of the magnetic fields across the entire territory of the USSR, again, that was him. And at present, instead of checking the instruments returning from the stratosphere, guiding planes over the frozen wastes where compasses go awry, or mapping the earth's magnetic fields, instead of dreaming of light being generated from the winds, what is he reduced to? Picking mushrooms and collecting plants. Today's a day off, he writes, I went out with a friend. We picked mushrooms, samples of plants, and we ate blackberries from the peat bogs . . . Bitter mockery. His friend, his student, Nikolay Zubov is sailing on the Kara Sea on the icebreaker *Sadko* (from the name of the Russian Sinbad, the subject of Rimsky-Korsakov's opera which he planned to see with Varvara on the evening of 8 January 1934 – a year and a half ago – a different era, a different world); he is going to set up a station on Solitude Island. I'm happy for him, writes Alexey Feodosievich. Like Schmidt, I expect he will try to forget me, but in his heart he must remember what I have done for him. We surrounded the entire Arctic with a network of expeditions. Like Zubov, I too dreamed of being part of one of them . . . Solitude Island in fact, that's where he is.

Back in 1925, he writes, I recommended bringing the weather forecasting services together in one big unified department, and in 1929 I succeeded. And one day my project of combining the weather forecasting services of the entire world will come about, of that I have no doubt. Here I've given two lectures on the topic of 'Science at the service of everyday life'. I talked about molecular sequencing and concluded with the right way and the wrong way to sweep a floor. The audience was fascinated. My life is very dispiriting because I have no one to talk to, it is a total solitude, everything I experience, I experience alone. Alexey Feodosievich does not have the same point of view at all as Yury Chirkov, who is enthralled by the intellectual brilliance of the little group that gravitates towards the library. But Chirkov is a young man full of optimism, and Wangenheim a neurasthenic who feels his life ebbing, now useless. I'm continuing to study foreign languages in fits and starts, he writes. Talking of solitude, I forgot to mention an animal: my little cat. We have grown very attached to one another. He has just jumped off my shoulder where he'd been quietly snoozing. He is well-behaved, affectionate and crafty, he knows when I'm about to eat, he comes up to me and starts to claw at my puttees. Once he went out of the open door, I looked for him for ages but he came back of his own accord. It may seem strange, but this playful little grey creature comforts me even though he messes up my papers or makes my table dirty with his mucky paws.

It is a total solitude. We dried the mushrooms, he writes. When you send me a parcel, put in a fine-tooth comb. We have to have our heads shorn here, but between shavings, I'd like to comb my hair, and the teeth in the comb I made are too far apart. It's such a shame to have to think about such things rather than important matters ... I'm struggling to remain strong. I'm wearing new shoes. I was afraid I'd have to keep the old ones which are very worn, but I've been given new ones which are one and a half sizes too big, but with socks and puttees they are all right. So I'm all kitted out, if they aren't stolen, which is what usually happens. We're preparing for the anniversary of the October Revolution, it's the second one I'll be celebrating without you and Eleonora, with an overwhelming sense of utter absurdity. I am very tired. I had a huge boil on my back, today's the first day I'm able to sit at my table to write. My right hand is a lot better, but now it's the left that is beginning to hurt. Tomorrow it will be one month since I sent my seventh letter to Stalin. Either my letters aren't reaching him, or they are not being read. Deep down I fear that no one cares about the truth.

There are no attempts at escape, or very few. The sixty kilometres that separate the principal island from the mainland form an almost insuperable barrier, whether the sea is thawed, from May to November, or frozen. And the men of the NKVD patrol the shores around Kem, opposite. However, in September of this year of 1935, there is one. Chirkov, newly disembarked from the *Udarnik*, describes it. The power station siren goes off, the dogs lead the pursuers down to the shore, the camp's small seaplane takes to the sky. If the fugitive tries to cross the inlet, he has almost no chance of avoiding detection. A storm blows up, forcing the sea search to be called off. After a week, the fugitive's body is found crushed amid a heap of tree trunks washed ashore by the storm. His name is Pavel Boreysha, he was a member of the Komsomol who had been appalled by the sight of those who had starved to death in Ukraine and had had the courage to write about it. He had been deported as a result. He too had sent a petition to Stalin, which had been read, because it earned him a transfer to a cruel penalty isolator.

I am utterly alone here, writes Alexey Feodosievich at the beginning of December 1935. I get on well with several of the men, but I am not close to anyone. I'm a misfit, a white crow. I sent my petition to Vyshinsky, I don't know what will come of it. It's the first time I have asked the prosecutor to review my case. Given that two years have gone by, I have high hopes. I'm convinced that if I remain alive, the Party will eventually clarify everything. It is just a matter of time. My faith in the Party remains unshaken, he writes on 24 December. Then, on 18 January: my petition has been filed under number 1726. There's a terrible storm blowing, the snow stings your eyes. I gave a lecture on the conquest of the stratosphere, there were people of all ages in the audience, from nine years old to the elderly, and they all listened attentively.

He is a white crow here. I am utterly alone here. You tell me you haven't received any letters for a long time, he says, but I write regularly. Why would anyone delay the post? During my walks, he writes, I talk to the moon and I ask it to give my greetings to my darlings. It shines on you at the same time as on me. Yesterday I saw a magnificent green aurora borealis. At first it was like a curtain rippling across the sky, then rays and rainbows. When you think about the altitude at which it is happening, probably over two hundred kilometres from Earth, and at what astonishing speed the rays are moving, you're struck by what a powerful phenomenon it is. I'm reading Fridtjof Nansen, he writes, *Farthest North*. He was also cut off from the world, but what wouldn't I give to swap places with him. After being forced to turn back on his walk to the North Pole, the Norwegian Nansen had spent an entire winter in a make-shift shelter on the Franz-Josef archipelago in northern Siberia. Wherever I look, writes Alexey Feodosievich, whatever I think about, everything seems gloomy, agonising, often desperate, the only glimmer in the darkness is you, my darlings. That star lights the way, and I won't give up, despite the overwhelming facts, despite the grim reality. I continue to hope that the darkness will be dispelled, that the Party will acknowledge the truth. And yet, my fifteen petitions addressed to the leaders remain unanswered ... Perhaps the petition I sent to Vyshinsky met the same fate. I bought some seal blubber, he adds.

Yesterday I saw a magnificent green aurora borealis. The days follow on from one another monotonously, each one is a desperate loss, drawing me closer to the end of my life, he says. My petition has been filed under number 1726 ... I am quietly continuing my Arctic research. When I immerse myself in my studies, I forget a little. Never in my life have I devoted so much time to trivial domestic details – that must be the meaning of 'rehabilitation through work' ... It's obvious that stupid jobs, cleaning toilets etc., are more useful to the Construction of the Soviet Union than finding answers to important scientific questions ... Furthermore, he writes, we should not try to analyse things that are beyond our understanding. This little grey creature, my cat, with his dirty paws, comforts me in my sadness. I had a reply to one of my enquiries about my eighth petition to Comrade Stalin: it was sent to the Central Committee secretariat on 15 November 1935. No result. I don't think there will be one, and I wrote to Dimitrov to no avail. You know, if someone had talked to me before 8 January about what I am forced to conclude now, I would have spat in his face and called him a liar and a slanderer.

In March, he writes, I gave ten lectures on the aurora borealis. I have seen several, mostly they are in the form of an arc, but once I saw curtains of green rays shimmering in the sky and undulating as if in the wind. I teach others things, but I myself am learning nothing, for lack of books on the subject. On the other hand, I read new books on the physics of the atomic nucleus with interest. I try to be outdoors as often as possible. On the 20th, I was able to measure the depth of the snow around the 'Kremlin'. Thanks to the boots you sent me I leaped around in the snow like a hare, and in some places it came right up to my waist. The average depth of the snow is seventy centimetres. This little note gives an insight both into the way Wangenheim's mind worked, focused on numbers and precise measurements rather than the imagination (admittedly circumstances did not lend themselves to fantasy), and into his despair at his enforced idleness. I've started to write a lecture on the eclipse of the sun that will take place on 19 June, he writes. I'm building a huge planetarium. I remember 1914, when the Academy of Sciences planned to send me to Feodosia to observe the full eclipse of the sun. I bought a suitcase and a whole lot of equipment, but four days before my departure I was called up, and instead of Feodosia, I found myself at the front.

I'm preparing for the eclipse of the sun that will take place on 19 June, he writes, I'm finishing the big planetarium, I'm doing technical drawings, and there's one question I can't get out of my mind: why can't I do this for my little Elia and for your students? In some places, especially where there are large numbers of regular prisoners, people listen attentively, avidly even, to my talks. For me it's a good exercise in making science understandable, I'm training myself to explain sometimes very complicated things in a way that is simple. I'm sending you two drawings of the aurora borealis for your students, he writes. I listened to the broadcast of the May Day parade on Red Square on the radio, and it made me feel so miserable that I went outside to stop myself from weeping. At the moment I'm studying Einstein's theory of relativity, he writes a month later, at the very beginning of June, and I feel capable of tackling these difficult questions. Soon Einstein's theory will be considered a 'Talmudist abstraction', and physicists referring to it as agents of a foreign conspiracy. *Life and Fate*, the great novel by Vasily Grossman, talks about it, among other things that are essential to understanding the twentieth century. Amid the debris of all his convictions, Alexey Feodosievich clings to that which does not founder – his love for his family and his mental stamina: he is capable, he is still capable of studying the theory of relativity. Long imprisoned by the ice, the spring bursts into life, the cuckoos start to sing, the frogs to croak in the hundreds of lakes and marshes dotted around the island, the seagulls are back and their screeching keeps him awake, the vegetation shoots up, cranberries, blueberries sprinkling the undergrowth with millions of coloured beads. But what is the use of spring? There is no night, the sun goes down, blots out the horizon to the north and rises again, making the clouds explode with all the colours of the spectrum. Wangenheim cannot be relied on to give colourful descriptions of the glories of nature, it is even curious that his love of drawing does not seem to go hand in hand with an acute sense of observation. The letters of Pavel Florensky written at the same time give us a much better idea of the celestial gems of the white nights: 'Last night, on returning from the "Kremlin", I was unable to tear myself away from the prodigious richness of the colours of the sky: purple, violet, lilac, pink, orange, gold, grey, scarlet, pale blue, blue-green and white: the interplay of all the colours in the sky streaked with long, thin layers of purple clouds.' 'The splendour of Claude Lorrain,' he adds, 'with much more richness and diversity of hues.' Rays fan out from the rims of the clouds and strike the surface of the sea, reminding him this time of Raphael's *Vision of Ezekiel*.

This all makes me feel like Radames in the last act of *Aida*, writes Alexey Feodosievich, but without Aida, and without a feeling of guilt. In this place we hear echoes of the joys of life and the triumph of the cause that is dear to me, but all at an inaccessible distance. I remember the years after the Revolution, when I used to give lectures in the towns and villages. How many talks did I give for the peasants on Soviet power, socialism! Enough, it would seem, to get me sent here. It is the irony of History. The observation of the eclipse was not a success, he writes on 20 July, in the morning the sky was very overcast and we were only able to see the second half of the phenomenon during brief sunny spells. A few days ago, I experienced a few highly emotional moments: I was told that I had authorisation to receive a visit, but, as I feared, they had muddled my name up with someone else's. I knew it, and yet I couldn't help feeling full of hope. I put in a petition to have my file rectified: they added, by mistake, paragraph 10 of article 58. All the other charges are trumped up too, naturally, but at least we should be spared bureaucratic errors. I don't know whether I'll receive satisfaction.

I have a big abscess under my arm, he writes, I don't know why, but here abscesses are common, apparently it's because of the weather. I don't understand, I can't believe what the others tell me, I'm desperately trying to hold on to my faith in the Soviet leadership and the Party. At the moment, on the radio I can hear the Kremlin bell tolling the twelve strokes of midnight, I can hear the car horns in Red Square. And two evenings ago, here I was, giving a lecture on life on Mars . . . I buy milk, carrots and cabbage. I have ninety-five roubles in my account. This is the third October Revolution anniversary that I'll be spending without you and Eleonora. I have to tidy up the 1,100 square metres of the museum and dust the thousands of exhibits on display. Liturgical objects, icons, psalters, antiphonaries, venerable bibles, manuscripts of ancient chronicles, the correspondence of Ivan the Terrible – some of the monastery's treasures had been hidden from the Chekists' greed and salvaged from the fire of 1923 and were kept in an 'anti-religious museum' housed in the former apartments and the archimandrite's chapel. As part of the Revolution anniversary celebrations, Wangenheim had to conduct guided tours. I've been put in charge of the history and art sections, he writes. For that, I receive 'Pot 2' rations, in other words I get an extra 800 grams of bread. Yesterday I draught-proofed the windows and walls of our cell; there were cracks everywhere. I'm going to be spending another winter here, I don't see any light shining in the depths of the night, I will have to spend another seven like this. This is the rest I've earned for the work I have done.

My faith in the Soviet leadership remains unshaken ... You know, he writes, it sometimes occurs to me that my devotion to the Party and to the construction of socialism has led me to where I am, and in keeping it intact I am becoming increasingly enslaved. That is the irony of History. The frozen rowanberries sprinkled with sugar are delicious. I found the time to draw a reindeer for Elia. Today, your birthday, he writes on 17 December, I thought of sending you a portrait of Comrade Stalin and a horse's head made of stone chippings. A funny birthday present ... Curiously, each time he makes a portrait of Stalin, he then does one of a domestic animal. In one week's time, he writes on 1 January 1937, it will be three years ... the first year I was certain that the truth would come out and this nightmare without rhyme or reason would end. The second year, certainty gave way to hope. And now the third year has passed and there is no certainty or hope any more, even though I have not abandoned my convictions, I still think that the leaders are not aware of my situation. Throughout these three years, I have battled in my heart not to allow myself to think ill of the Soviet authorities or of the leaders, not to blame them for what is happening. What will the fourth year bring? For us, personally, probably not a lot of joy. Before this fourth year is over, the poor man will be dead, massacred along with a thousand others in the depths of a forest at night.

Yesterday we celebrated the New Year, he continues. At around eleven-thirty, I finished washing the museum floor. Then, I began a drawing for Elishka. It's my present to you, my darlings. At ten to midnight, the head of the museum called me into his room, we drank a cup of coffee and listened to the broadcast from Red Square, and we were both thinking that our families were listening to the same thing at the same time as us, and were perhaps remembering us. Then we went to bed. I sent my petition to Yezhov, but without any hope. A petition to Nikolay Yezhov! It's like looking for sympathy from a shark ... the 'Bloody Dwarf' (he was barely one metre fifty tall) had taken over as People's Commissar for Internal Affairs from Genrikh Yagoda, whom he'd had shot. Under his 'reign' from 1937 to 1938, the Great Terror, permanently associated with his name, was unleashed (in Russian this period of great purges is called the *Yezhovshchina* – literally the times of Yezhov), making the repression of the preceding years seem almost banal. Not surprisingly, this servile perpetrator of the Stalinist madness ended up being executed, reportedly asking for his master and executioner to be told that he would die with his name on his lips ... I sent my petition to Yezhov, writes Wangenheim on 11 January 1937, I did it without any hope, but my conscience demands that I try this avenue too.

He is surprised to find his name is mentioned in a book on the stratosphere published in 1936, whereas in others, published in 1934, it had been removed. I am accustomed to everything being forgotten or distorted, he says. It is the second month of the year, he writes in February, and this all feels as if it's just a horrible nightmare. It is certain that my letter to Yezhov won't have a positive outcome. But there's no negative outcome either for the time being. Don't you do anything. Let things happen as has been decided by someone, despite the absurdity of it all. I remember the early months, when they threatened my family. The present ordeal is enough. Water freezes in the room. I draught-proofed and even plastered the walls. The stove works perfectly. My hand isn't too bad, but the inflammation isn't going down. I can chop wood, which I wasn't able to do before. I heard that Otto Yulyevich has been honoured again. Instead of three additional letters, I was only allowed two. Yesterday I ran a temperature and I wasn't able to go outside. I'm studying the monastic economy of the Solovetsky Islands. I found an icon depicting two angels whipping a woman. Sometimes I find extraordinary things in storerooms. I still feel cold in my soul. It's taken them three years to recognise that paragraph 10 of article 58, which was applied to me, was an error, he writes in April. I have 58.7, sabotage, but not 58.10, anti-Soviet propaganda. Until now, I have always been told I was charged with both, but it wasn't until a few days ago that I found out I only had one charge. That doesn't make much difference, but it's fairly typical: you have to wait three years to find out why you've been condemned . . .

All this is just one long nightmare. You ask what was the outcome of my letter to Yezhov: nothing, of course, as I expected. It's already something not to have been punished. You can imagine how I felt when I learned about the fate of the *Severny polyus-1*, he writes in August. 'North Pole 1' is a drifting base, in other words a small section of an ice floe carrying basic instruments and drifting with the movement of the ice. Ivan Papanin, an 'Arctic hero' like Schmidt, was dropped off near the North Pole in May along with three companions, and for eight months he will travel nearly 3,000 kilometres without moving. Preparations for the expedition got under way when I was president of the Soviet Committee for the Second International Polar Year, writes Alexey Feodosievich. I'm very worried about your financial situation, he says on 19 September, how much are you managing to earn? It's so painful feeling helpless . . . You don't need to send me money every month, or send just one rouble instead of three. I have 260 in my account, which is enough to last me two years. I never let slip an opportunity to write to you. If you don't receive any letters for a while, don't worry, it absolutely doesn't mean that something has happened to me. I write to you twice a month and your letters are reaching me. I'm trying to remain philosophical, but unfortunately my nerves don't always allow it. What's more, I'm morally inflexible, that's another shortcoming that causes me to suffer. If it weren't for that inflexibility, everything would have been easier, but I don't want to lose it. I have no doubt that History will restore my good name . . .

My dear little daughter, he writes to Eleonora at the end of September, I shall not be able to send you my drawings for a while, but I hope you'll send me yours. Does he already know that he is going to be transferred to the mainland? Probably, but then why does he ask his daughter to carry on sending him drawings? Does he think that the administration of the BBK, the White Sea Canal camps, currently in charge of the prison on the Solovetsky Islands will forward them? Did you get your second Arctic fox? he asks. Did you receive the bullfinch and *varakusha* nests? The *varakusha* is a bird with a blue back and a browny-orange breast that's a little like a sort of thrush. What are you doing at the moment? How are your music lessons going? My little cat is still very well behaved, we're good friends. This letter is the last that he will write. At the end of October, recalls Yury Chirkov, a very long list was read out in the Solovki 'Kremlin', almost 1,200 names, who were given two hours to gather together their meagre belongings and say goodbye to their friends. Then the convoy, walking four abreast, passed under the Holy Gate leading to the port. Chirkov recognised in passing several of his close friends, Pavel Florensky, the Orthodox priest with an encyclopaedic mind, Grigory Kotlyarevsky, the former head of the library, Pyotr Ivanovich Weigel, who had taught him German and who shouted by way of farewell two lines from Goethe's *Faust*: *Auf, bade, Schüler, unverdrossen / Die irdische Brust im Morgenrot* (Arise, young man, and bathe undaunted/ Your earthly breast in dawn's first red), and 'Wangenheim, in a black coat and sea-lion shapka hat. They spotted me and nodded their heads (their hands were holding suit-cases).' The convoy set sail for Kem, under a low, grey sky. Nothing more was heard of it. It took sixty years before persistent investigators from the Memorial Research Centre eventually uncovered its story and found out its destination.

A few days after the convoy's departure, Chirkov noted in a fairly Shakespearian manner, on 9 November, that an extraordinary aurora borealis appeared in the sky: not the usual green curtains, but purple arcs dancing in the night. 'Several people interpreted it as a disturbing omen.'

III

I

At the end of October 1937, 1,116 prisoners embark for Kem and from that moment all trace of them is lost for sixty years. It is a dismal autumn day, says Chirkov, the ship sets sail, its trail fades into the grey water, and for a long while it is still visible heading westwards, towards Kem, under a plume of vapour that mingles with the low, grey cloud, and then all that can be seen is the steam, then nothing. (There were probably several ships, or several voyages – I doubt whether over 1,000 people can be crammed into the *Udarnik,* even deep in the hold.) Those 1,116 captives vanished with the steam from the ship into the bloody night of what today we call the Great Terror. Are we capable of imagining the horror of the endless wait, for years on end? Varvara, Alexey Feodosievich's wife, receives no more letters. He told her not to worry if she didn't hear from him for a while, that it didn't mean something had happened to him. So, at first, she tries not to worry. Then, as the months go by and the silence persists, she starts trying to obtain information, but draws a blank. In May 1939 she appeals to Beria, who has replaced Yezhov at the head of the NKVD: 'All my petitions have gone unanswered. I request that you let me know where my husband is at present, as a matter of urgency.' On 28 June, she writes to the Prosecutor General of the USSR, the department headed by Vyshinsky, and it is they who eventually reply that Alexey Feodosievich is alive, that in 1937 his case was reviewed and that he has been sentenced to a further ten years without the right to send or receive letters, and transferred to a faraway camp whose name cannot be disclosed.

Ten years without being allowed to send or receive any correspondence – we now know that means death. But at the time, people do not know that, or rather, since death is everywhere – 'The stars of the dead stand above us,' wrote Akhmatova in *Requiem* – it can hide behind this formula as behind any words, any face. But people probably do not imagine that on top of the Soviet state's extreme brutality there is also the barefaced lie, that this Moloch that devours hundreds of thousands of lives also acts like a child caught misbehaving, that those who have no scruples about mass murder are afraid their crimes will be discovered. And so Varvara Ivanovna does not lose hope. Ten years – ten years without news – is an unbearably long time, but perhaps she will see her husband again one day. World war breaks out, with the USSR initially on the side of the predators alongside the Nazis, then, on 22 June 1941, Germany invades the

Soviet Union and marches to the gates of Moscow. Evacuated to Magnitogorsk, in the Urals, Varvara takes her husband's belongings with her, so he'll be able to retrieve them on his return. The war is over, she is awarded a medal for having courageously defended her school during an air raid; she will even receive the Order of Lenin in 1949. No doubt, like many ordinary Soviet citizens, she thought that the appalling sacrifices made during what was called 'the Great Patriotic War', the heroism of the people, of the people-soldiers but also of just the people, the million civilian deaths during the twenty-eight-month siege of Leningrad, would earn this people – this *narod* in whose name supposedly everything was done, everything was accomplished – a little freedom, or in any case the enjoyment of simple things, a father being reunited with his daughter, for example. A father whose belongings are still waiting for him, repatriated from Magnitogorsk to Moscow in spring 1944. A daughter who is now fifteen years old, who is advised to change her surname so as to be able to pursue her studies more easily, to take her mother's name, Kurguzova, but who refuses to do so. If Varvara Ivanovna thinks this, as is likely, we know – we who also know what 'ten years without being allowed to send or receive any correspondence' means – that she is horribly mistaken. Stalin, revelling in the glory of the decisive battle fought in the city that bears his name, in the taking of Berlin and victory, in the carving up of the world at Yalta, with Roosevelt and Churchill, Stalin has absolutely no intention of showing himself to be kind-hearted: that would be to push his nature too far, and he still has so many scores to settle with spies, traitors, saboteurs, antisocial elements, former prisoners of war, dubious nationalities (the Jews in particular), people who believed that the Internationale would unite the human race ... Why should he deprive himself? He has made such a success of everything ...

Except that he eventually dies, on 5 March 1953. 'A great god, the idol of the twentieth century, had died ...', writes Grossman ironically in *Everything Flows*. And he describes the hysterical weeping in the factories, the streets and the schools, but also the jubilation of the millions of prisoners in the camps, the murmur that rises up from the columns of *zeks* trudging through the Arctic darkness beside the glacial ocean: 'He's gone!' If Alexey Feodosievich had lived long enough to see this day, if in 1937 he really had been sentenced to ten additional years in the camp and had survived (this sentence, added to the first, would have run until 1954), would he too have whispered joyfully to his neighbour 'He's gone'? It is not certain. Would he have continued to maintain, desperately, crazily, his faith in the Party and the Soviet state, to believe that Stalin was unaware of the unheard-of suffering under his rule? That is not certain either, and we can in any case hope not. But at this point, I should mention something disturbing; shocking, even: with the last letter he sent to his wife, in September 1937, he enclosed a little portrait of Stalin made of stone chippings. I held that portrait in my hands, in the Memorial

Research Centre in St Petersburg. Measuring around fifteen by twelve centimetres, the idol of the masses is depicted in three-quarter view, against an ochre background. He is wearing a grey pea jacket buttoned up to the neck, his hair thick, the moustache of a janissary. It is the only object that his daughter Eleonora bequeathed to us in her lifetime, Irina Flighe, director of Memorial tells me. She could not bear the idea that there had been this – this thing – in the last message from her father, along with the mention of the Arctic foxes, the bullfinches and the little cat.

Why did Alexey Feodosievich send that portrait? His reasons I do not know, and no one ever will. Did he still have faith in Stalin, even though he had not replied to a single one of his letters? Throughout these three years, he wrote in December 1936, I've battled not to allow myself to think ill of the Soviet authorities and of the leaders, not to blame them for what is happening. What will the fourth year bring? You could feel his conviction wavering, and that the vestiges of his faith were more like an antidepressant which he forced himself to take each day to stop himself from going to pieces. So does he send this portrait because he can foresee the fate that awaits him – you won't be receiving any letters for a while, he says to his wife and daughter – and this is the last thing he can do to protect his family: show that he is a good Communist, a dutiful servant? Let things happen as has been decided by someone, he wrote in February 1937, despite the absurdity of it all. I remember the early months, when they threatened my family. So they threatened to attack his wife and his daughter, his 'little star'. This fear might explain his repeated protestations of loyalty to the Party, for he knew that all his letters would of course pass through the hands of the censor, that everything he wrote could help build a new case against him and deny him his freedom once he'd served his sentence. Worse still, they could be used against the woman and little girl who were the only lights shining in his darkness. Wherever I look, he wrote in February 1936, whatever I think about, everything seems dark, grim, often desperate, the only light in the darkness is you, my darlings. The fear of seeing his family persecuted was not only in his imagination: by virtue of the NKVD's 'operational order no. 00486', 40,000 'wives or concubines' were arrested and deported in 1937–1938 (it was stipulated that those who had informed on their husbands should be spared), and their children placed in state orphanages. And so it is possible, or probable, that it was with the slender hope of shielding Varvara and Eleonora – the wife and daughter of an enemy of the people – from the harshness of the secret police, that he sent them the handmade portrait of the dictator, hoping it might give them its protection in the same way as the religious icons of the past.

'Stalin's death was not part of any plan,' writes Vasily Grossman in *Everything Flows*, 'he died without instructions from any higher authority. Stalin died without receiving personal instructions from Comrade Stalin himself. In the freedom and capriciousness of death there was something explosive, something hostile to the innermost essence of the Soviet State.' With this sudden freedom, he says, 'the State was shaken, just as it had been shaken by the shock of the German invasion of 22 June 1941.' One of the consequences of this disruption, of this tremor that had shaken up the leadership on the death of the dictator, was the process of reviewing convictions and the rehabilitation of the victims. On 29 April 1956, the military judge Major General Ye. Varskoy, Deputy Prosecutor General, made a submission to the Military Collegium of the Supreme Court of the Soviet Union. It stated that the sentences handed down to Wangenheim on 27 March 1934 by the Collegium of the OGPU (ten years' camp) and on 9 October 1937 by the NKVD Special Troika of the Leningrad region (capital punishment) could not be ratified and should be repealed. (Each troika was a commission of three members representing the NKVD, the Prosecutor-General and the regional Party who meted out swift sentences to those accused of political crimes in their absence.) The evidence against Wangenheim, argued the major general (that was his rank in the military magistrature), confirming the existence of a counter-revolutionary sabotage organisation of which he was alleged to be the leader, could not be upheld insofar as the surviving witnesses had since retracted their statements. Some testimonies were reportedly obtained under torture. Wangenheim himself, having admitted at the beginning of the investigation his leading role in the counter-revolutionary organisation, subsequently withdrew his confession. The checks carried out in the archives of the Ministry of the Interior of the Soviet Union and of the KGB yielded no evidence of any alleged espionage activity; on the contrary, they confirmed that the authorities had cracked down on the accused prior to 1917 for his participation in the revolutionary movement. In witness whereof the deputy Prosecutor General requested the repeal of the OGPU's decision of 27 March 1934 and that of the Special Troika of 9 October 1937, and that the investigation be annulled.

It is now 29 April 1956, two months since Khrushchev delivered, before the closed session of the Twentieth Congress of the Communist Party, his famous 'Secret Speech' denouncing Stalin's 'personality cult' and crimes (well, not all, far from it; not the campaigns of mass terror; nor those in which he, Khrushchev had been involved). Varvara finally learns that her husband, arrested twenty-two years earlier, and from whom she has received no news for nineteen years, had not been sentenced in 1937 to ten additional years of camp without the right to send or receive any correspondence, as she had been told, but to death. This April day is the first when she will no longer be waiting for him to return. His belongings, which she had kept in their home at 7 Dokuchayev pereulok and carted to Magnitogorsk, then brought back to Moscow once the German threat had moved away from the capital, will no longer be of any use. Momentous events have taken place, there has been a world war, and he was dead. Nazi Germany has been defeated, the Russian empire has extended to Eastern Europe, and he has been dead for a long time. The 'Little father of the peoples' whose portrait she has in ochre, grey and brown stone chippings is dead, and he, Alexey Feodosievich, has been dead for sixteen years unbeknown to her, in a place she does not and will never know: the Soviet state has the magnanimity to acknowledge its deplorable mistakes, to annul *post mortem* a capital execution, but not to disclose the scenes of its crimes (of its 'mistakes'). She learns simultaneously that he was sentenced to death and that he is officially innocent. The truth eventually came out, as Wangenheim, at first, had never ceased to believe, and then to hope, with an increasingly tremulous faith – but he is no longer here to experience this moral liberation. She finds out that he was sentenced to death, but the Prosecutor General of the Soviet Union has requested that this sentence be repealed ... and effectively, on 10 August 1956, the colonel-judge P. Likhachev, president of the Military Collegium of the Soviet Union Supreme Court, signed a rehabilitation order: 'The decision of the OGPU Collegium of 27 March 1934 and the decision of the NKVD Special Troika of the Leningrad region of 9 October 1937 concerning Wangenheim, Alexey Feodosievich are annulled. The case is closed for lack of a *corpus delicti*. Wangenheim, Alexey Feodosievich is rehabilitated posthumously.'

The death is annulled. The case is closed. But not entirely. The Soviet state hasn't invented the Resurrection of the Dead, but another great mystery, the multiplication of the dead. For, to complete the macabre comedy, one year later, on 26 April 1957, an entirely different administrative body, the registry office of Leningrad's Kuybyshev district, delivers to Varvara Ivanovna a 'death certificate' (*svidetelstvo o smerti*) stating that Wangenheim, Alexey Feodosievich died on 17 August 1942, of peritonitis. Under 'place of death', 'town, district', 'region, republic', there is only a line in purple ink. Thus the chaos of belated half-truths and lies meant that prisoner Wangenheim, who set sail with 1,115 others at the end of October 1937 for Kem and then on to an unknown destination, now has, twenty years later, a brand new innocence conferred on him, and two deaths on two different dates and in two places equally unknown.

2

On 30 July 1937, the 'Bloody Dwarf' Nikolay Yezhov, People's Commissar for Internal Affairs, had signed NKVD Operational Order 00447, unleashing the wave of political violence that would last sixteen months and go down in History as The Great Terror, as opposed to the Terror that could be called ordinary, which had until then been the day-to-day norm. During those sixteen terrible months of the *Yezhovshchina*, some 750,000 people were shot (an average of 1,600 executions a day during the last five months of 1937), and nearly as many sent to the prison camps. Some 750,000 shot – that is half the number of French soldiers who died during World War I, in less than half the time. Some 750,000 is not an approximate figure, it is the total of the statistics compiled by the NKVD eighth department ('Statistical Department') itself: slightly higher, according to the Memorial Research Centre, to take into account the unrecorded executions in excess of the quotas. This astounding total does not include the many 'natural deaths' from hunger, cold and exhaustion in the prison camps of the Gulag during this period.

Operational Order 00447 was aimed at the 'former kulaks, socially harmful elements, members of anti-Soviet parties, former White Guards, members of religious sects and of the clergy, criminals and other anti-Soviet elements', in other words a large number of very diverse people (church officials, Mensheviks, revolutionary socialists, cattle thieves, and that Chekhovian category of *byvshie*, the 'people of the past', including both poets and landowners). Anyone, in fact, depending on the whim of the state security agents. Sentencing quotas were set for each region or republic, in order to mercilessly get rid of all the vermin, to 'put an end to their activities once and for all'. The sentences were divided into 'first category' (death) and 'second category' (being sent to a correctional labour camp, generally for ten years). So for Moscow, order 00447 required 5,000 first-category sentences and 30,000 second (it was Khrushchev who had suggested these numbers); for the Leningrad region, 4,000 and 10,000 respectively. Order 00447 was very comprehensive, omitting no region or sub-region; some were generously endowed with corpses, others sparingly (5,000 for the Sea of Azov and the Black Sea region, 100 only for the Kalmyks or the Komi, which inevitably led to jealousy). It covered every single detail. (For example, point VI.2 specifies: 'First-category sentences are executed in the places and on the dates determined by the head of the NKVD of the region or the republic. Executions will take place in conditions of utmost secrecy both as to the place and the date.)' The total requested was a little over 75,000 executions.

For once the plan was to be superseded and the number of 'first-category convictions' under order 00447 was multiplied by five. In order better to 'uproot', 'extract', 'purge' and 'annihilate', each regional NKVD head had asked for the quota of dead allocated to them to be increased, and Stalin never failed to encourage this sinister emulation among his hunting dogs, placing a big 'approved' in red pencil on the applications presented to him – which, in this case, were diligently read. And the mass graves did not open up only before those sentenced under order 00447; there were still, as great purveyors of death, the 'national operations' targeting German, Polish, Latvian, Estonian, Greek, Romanian and Korean nationals, Soviet citizens who had worked on the Harbin railway line in Manchuria, suspected of being Japanese spies, and lastly all immigrants, even political refugees, even members of foreign Communist parties. Operational Order 00693, point I: 'I order the immediate arrest of all immigrants whatever the reason or circumstances of their being in the USSR. They are to be subjected to a full and thorough interrogation.' In each region, the NKVD–Prosecutor-General–Party 'troikas', specially created commissions of assassins, were tasked with issuing sentences as on a production line, often several hundred a day, with immediate effect.

The *zek* Wangenheim unwittingly fell under the

grindstone of this paranoid people-crushing machine. Serving his ten-year labour camp sentence, he dreamed less and less often that justice would be meted out to him, and believed in any case that he would be freed in 1944. These are exactly, as we are able to reconstruct them today, the different stages of the process that resulted – after numerous directives, memoranda, statements, red tape of all sorts, signatures and rubber stamps – in a bullet in the back of the head. Order 00447 set the quota of death sentences 'earmarked' for the NKVD labour camps at 10,000. Regarding this figure, on 16 August 1937, Yezhov told Zakovsky, head of the Leningrad region NKVD, that 'the quota allocated to you for the Solovki camp is 1,200' (this initial quota would in fact be raised to just over 1,800). Major Apeter, the Solovki chief, then drew up his list and compiled for each of the names on it a 'file' reduced as per instructions to a simple summary – civil status, sentence being served. He sent that to the special troika in Leningrad, which, in nearly all cases, decided on death. And this entire process was 'with no further investigation or new accusations', as was underlined in 1956 in the petition for rehabilitation presented by the deputy Prosecutor General. And naturally, without the accused being informed that their case was being reviewed, or their sentence. Mikhail Frinovsky, Yezhov's deputy (who would be shot alongside him), was adamant on this point in a memorandum to all the regional NKVD chiefs: 'Do not inform the first-category individual of the sentence inflicted. I repeat: do not inform them.' And, on 9 October 1937, the Leningrad region NKVD Special Troika, comprising Leonid Zakovsky, president, his deputy Vladimir Garin and the prosecutor Boris Pozern, 'HAVING TAKEN COGNIZANCE OF case number 120, Wangenheim Alexey Feodosievich, Russian, Soviet citizen, born in 1881 in the village of Krapivno, Chernigov province of the Ukrainian SSR, son of a noble and landowner, university education, teacher, last place of work: Hydro-meteorological Department of the USSR, former member of the Bolshevik Communist Party, former officer in the Tsarist army, sentenced to ten years' labour camp by decision of the OGPU Collegium on 27 March 1934, DECREE: to be shot (*Rasstrelyat*).'

It then remains for Major Apeter on the Solovetsky Islands to round up the condemned men and deliver them to the executioners. The management of such huge numbers about to go to their deaths gave the NKVD a logistical headache, just imagine; so the 1,825 prisoners the troika sentenced 'to be shot' were divided into three groups: one of 200, who would be killed there on the Solovetsky Islands, another of 509, transferred to the Leningrad region for execution, and a third of 1,116, which included Wangenheim. This was the convoy that Yury Chirkov watched leaving on a grey day in October 1937. The NKVD captain Mikhail Matveyev was tasked with picking up the condemned men in Kem. You must 'proceed with their execution according to the instructions given to you in person', states the order signed by the NKVD chief Zakovsky and Lieutenant Alexandr Yegorov, commanding officer of the third operative section of the State Security. 'You will report back on your return.' What are these instructions? What macabre terminus was planned for the convoy? As we have seen, order 00447 prescribes 'the utmost secrecy concerning both the place and the date of the executions'. In the case of the convoy from the Solovetsky Islands, this secret will remain intact for sixty years, until 1997. Varvara Ivanovna will die in 1977 without knowing where or how or in what circumstances her husband was killed. Perhaps it was for the best. It is thanks to the dogged perseverance of some mavericks from the Memorial Research Centre that we know today how the meteorologist and his companions in suffering met their end.

3

The rest of the story was told to me by two of the three people who, after a lengthy investigation, eventually discovered the place and the circumstances of the executions: Irina Flighe and Yury Dmitriev – the third, Veniamin Iofe, has since died. Before coming to their story, though, I would like to make something clear: the executioners were meticulous and obsessed with secrecy but they were also bureaucratic, they were expeditious but they kept records; to explain their methods and practice (a word which here means killings and mass killings), it seems to me that you have to be meticulous too, and bureaucratic up to a point. Give the dates, ranks and signatures at the bottom of official documents, when they are known. At the risk of bogging down the text, perhaps. Expose their vocabulary, the categories, the words they used to describe the mass murder operation of which they were the agents. It is not devoid of interest to know that death was quantified in quotas, and called 'first-category sentence'. We need these details because they make us aware of a mass-murder operation that was also a scrupulous bureaucracy, and also because those names, ranks, dates and documents, all those 'details', were excavated by researchers and activists, campaigning researchers like Irina and Yury, from the secrecy in which the killers wanted them to remain buried. They are war booty.

Irina Flighe is director of the Memorial Research Centre in St Petersburg. Slim, animated, passionate, only putting down the telephone to have a smoke (although she's perfectly capable of juggling both), she exudes that selfless enthusiasm that sometimes is the beauty, so little appreciated nowadays, of the activist's face. Her world, Memorial, a labyrinthine apartment at the back of a courtyard in Rubinstein Street, its walls plastered with posters, shelves piled with brochures, reports and files on which forgotten cups of coffee or tea sit, ancient typewriters that have typed samizdats. It reminds me of the political HQs I've known in the past, where we devoted ourselves to less honourable causes. 'Through a friend of Antonina Sochina', she says (Antonina is the elderly woman who makes jams described at the very beginning of this book, in whose house I discovered the drawings and pressed flowers that Alexey Feodosievich sent his daughter), 'through a friend of Antonina who had access to the KGB archives in Arkhangelsk, we knew that the Leningrad troika had pronounced 1,825 death sentences in October 1937, but that was all we knew – what happened next was a mystery, as if the condemned had vanished into thin air. At the beginning of the

1990s, there were around one hundred people, descendants of those who disappeared in 1937, who were seeking answers to this mystery. The most energetic badgered the FSB (successor to the KGB, which had replaced the NKVD), the less energetic badgered us. Each year we would meet up on the Solovetsky Islands, for the Days of Remembrance, in June. We'd take the train and the boat together, we slept in shared dormitories. There was a collective energy. We had a feeling that we would succeed – and we have.

'At first, the most plausible theory was that the executions had taken place on the Solovetsky Islands themselves. But in June 1990, Chirkov's widow brought us her husband's unpublished manuscript' (Yury Chirkov, who had only finally been released on Stalin's death, had perished in 1988, before finishing his memoirs; curiously, he had become a meteorologist, like Wangenheim, holder of the chair of meteorology and climate science at the Timiryazev Agricultural Academy in Moscow), 'and in it we found a mention of the departure of the convoy for Kem, in October. That also matched evidence found on the islands, which seemed to suggest a mass departure on 17 October, for example this inscription carved into a wooden windowsill: "180 from Leningrad, accused of Trotskyist counter-revolutionary activities, were prisoners here from 12.11.36 to 17.10.37", or this one, on a wall on Anzer Island: "205 KRTD (Trotskyist counter-revolutionary activities) left on 17.10.37 for the unknown". And that also bore out the hunch of Veniamin Iofe, a former *zek* himself, who thought that executions on such a massive scale could not take place on the islands, because they couldn't have been kept secret in such a small space.

'Then we focused our search on different potential places – Kem, Arkhangelsk – to no avail. But each new scrap of information brought us closer to the truth. Everyone got involved, each false lead was quickly identified and dropped. Sergey Krivenko, a Moscow member of Memorial, managed to retrieve from the St Petersburg FSB the "accompanying notes" which Major Apeter handed over to Captain Matveyev with the condemned prisoners. There is nothing else on this Matveyev in St Petersburg, other than the mention of a reward – a gold watch – he was given for having efficiently carried out a mass execution: probably our convoy. But around this time (1996) a former KGB colonel, Lukin, published a self-justifying book in which he mentioned Matveyev, disclosing that for this operation, which he handled so smoothly, his rear base had been the town of Medvezhegorsk, in Karelia.'

Medvezhegorsk – 'bear mountain' – was the 'capital', if the word can be used, of the complex of camps built for the White Sea Canal project. Given the number of *bichi* – former intellectuals – deported to these camps, it was also, as one of them wrote, 'the capital of the Russian intelligentsia in the 1930s'. Nowadays it is a small town where one has no wish to linger. Just outside the town, you pass the high wooden fences, watchtowers and barbed wire of the 'zone', vestiges of the Gulag. In the centre, on Dzerzhinsky Street, is the high, peeling façade with broken windows of what was once the grand hotel built to accommodate Stalin, who came in 1933 to inaugurate the canal named after him. It is home to a covered market and the little museum. In front of it, the statue of Kirov and a T-34 tank commemorate the liberation from the Germano-Finnish occupation. A few rusty cranes, coal heaps and log piles: this is the port, on Lake Onega. All of these (with the mud-spattered Ladas and Zhigulis bumping over the potholed streets, the tall, thin chimneys of the boiler rooms, the overhead central-heating pipes that straddle the roads) make up a horribly Soviet landscape. The prettiest thing in Medvezhegorsk is the timber train station, a sort of railway dacha built in 1916 on the Murmansk line, which has miraculously survived World Wars I and II and the civil war. And seen countless convoys of slaves pass through. Many ghosts haunt its platforms. And so it became clear that we had to concentrate our search on Medvezhegorsk, explains Irina.

And it was precisely in Medvezhegorsk a few years earlier that Ivan Chukhin, a former colonel of the militia who had become a deputy in the Duma and a Memorial activist investigating the history of the construction of the canal, had come across the file for the prosecution in 1939 of two local camp chiefs, Alexandr Shondysh and Ivan Bondarenko, and of Captain Matveyev. (How long it seems since the 1990s, when the archives of the KGB/FSB were accessible and when a Memorial activist could be a deputy in the Duma.) In 1996, Chukhin died in a car accident, but Irina Flighe and Veniamin Iofe, who had come from St Petersburg, came across his research at the same time as they met Yury

Dmitriev, who was his assistant. Shondysh, Bondarenko and Matveyev had been accused of 'abuse of power' in conducting a mass execution, i.e. that of the Solovki convoy. The year 1939 was the period when Stalin claimed suddenly to have discovered the excesses of the Great Terror and sought to re-establish 'socialist legality', causing a few expiatory heads to roll, starting with Yezhov's. The three bastards charged with abuse of power were not condemned for having executed more than 1,000 people in cold blood, they were even rewarded for that, but they were criticised for not having abided by the rules, for treating those they were taking to the slaughter a little brutally. Shondysh and Bondarenko tried to shift the blame on to Matveyev. Without success, since they were to be sentenced to death and executed, whereas Matveyev got off with ten years, of which he served less than three.

It is time to introduce Mikhail Matveyev, NKVD executioner, one of those insane individuals who thrive in the secret police of dictatorships, a loathsome type who is to be found in the Gestapo, in the gangs of torturers of the Chilean or Argentinian military juntas or, more recently, among the henchmen of Tripoli or Damascus. It is by his hand – since it is a point of honour with him not to delegate the task of killing, for he never tires of blood – it is by his hand that Alexey Feodosievich Wangenheim will die. Doubtless it is easy to decide that a man known to be an executioner looks like a nasty piece of work, but frankly there is something unquestionably repulsive about his drooping cheeks and mouth, thick neck and pointed nose in the police mugshots taken in 1939. He was born in 1892, completed only two years of elementary studies and became an assistant locksmith at the Vulcan factory, but that was not his vocation: his fingers itched to trigger more than lock catches. The civil war saw him take part in the storming of the Winter Palace (which was in no way the heroic event depicted by Eisenstein), but it was as head of executions, a position that had a future, that he joined the secret police in 1918. In recognition of his work, which he performed with zeal (he was certainly no 'saboteur'), he received honours that bore the names of guns: Browning, Walther. Gold watches, Radiola radios. Rewards for an executioner. So at Kem he took charge of the convoy of 1,116 condemned prisoners from the Solovetsky Islands – they would be only 1,111 by the end of the voyage, one having died on the way, and four others having been required for the purpose of an investigation. He loaded them on to cattle trucks bound for Medvezhegorsk, in several contingents, the local prison having a capacity for just 300 people.

When Matveyev is interrogated in 1939, his replies are chilling. During the first round of executions, on 27 October, one prisoner who had managed to conceal a knife attempted to escape. So he perfects a procedure to avoid any nasty surprises. In Medvezhegorsk, the detainee is first taken into a hut where his identity is checked and he is stripped naked on the pretext of a medical examination, then into a second, adjoining hut where his hands are bound and his feet shackled, and lastly into a third where, if he appears stubborn, he is stunned with a sort of purpose-made club before being thrown on to a truck. Twenty to twenty-five prisoners per truck, covered with a tarpaulin on which the guards sit. Matveyev is not satisfied with the working conditions: he only has three or four guards per truck whereas the norm is eight plus a dog. He requests additional trucks, and instead of a truck he is sent tyres. The execution site is 'in the forest', no more specific location – there is almost nothing but forest around Medvezhegorsk. They dig deep trenches and throw in the condemned men, turning them face down and then shooting them with a bullet in the back of the head. Not they, but Matveyev in person. When he is asked if he has seen some of his men beating up the prisoners, he replies that it has indeed happened, but that he hadn't been able to see it because he was below, in the trench, with his Nagant gun. From time to time, when he is tired, when he wants to relax or smoke a cigarette, he clambers out and entrusts the task to his deputy, Lieutenant Alafer, but overall, it is he who is at the end of the chain, his boots in the blood-soaked mud awash with brains. Each day, or rather each night – because these things take place at night, on 27 October 1937 and from 1 to 4 November (the four-day hiatus having served to perfect the escape prevention procedure) – he dispatches between 200 and 250 counter-revolutionaries. And furthermore, he has to sign the certificates confirming that each sentence has been carried out. In short, he works flat out. His gold watch is well deserved.

4

By spring 1997, Irina Flighe sums up, we knew that there were 1,111 executions and that they took place in the forest close to Medvezhegorsk. And we even knew that the prison was around nineteen kilometres from the mass graves, because in the file on the 1939 trial Matveyev mentions this figure, complaining about the state of the roads to emphasise the difficulty of his 'job'. There aren't many roads out of Medvezhegorsk, but in any case, we knew that the one we were interested in was the one heading eastwards, towards Povenets and locks seven and eight of the canal, because at one point a truck broke down precisely because of the poor state of the road, and also because the truck was dilapidated, and Matveyev said that he was afraid the villagers of Pindushi might hear something – the prisoners' shouting or NKVD escorts swearing. Now Pindushi is on the Povenets road. So, the execution site had to be somewhere between Pindushi and Povenets.

Our present guide is Yury Dmitriev, one of those characters

you only find in Russia. I meet him for the first time in a hut inside a disused industrial zone surrounded by high walls, on the outskirts of Petrozavodsk, Karelia's capital. Rusty gantries, mountains of used tyres, twisted pipework, heaps of old asbestos, wrecked cars, beneath low clouds that seem to graze the brick chimneys: Yury is the guard of this place that epitomises the sense of abandonment characteristic of countless urban and suburban Russian landscapes. Emaciated, grey beard and hair scraped back in a ponytail, wearing an old army fatigue jacket, he strolls amid the wreckage like a cross between a Holy Fool and an old Pomorye pirate. 'In 1989,' he says, 'by chance, a mechanical digger unearthed a pile of human bones. The local officials, the military leaders and the Prosecutor's office – the whole world came to have a look, no one knew what to do, no one wanted to take responsibility. If you don't have the time, I said, I'll handle it. It took two years to prove that these were victims of the "repressions" (as these massacres are called, *repressiya* in Russian). We buried them in the former cemetery in Petrozavodsk. After the ceremony, my father told me that his father had been arrested and shot in '38. Until then, they'd told me that my grandfather had died, that was all. Then I felt the urge to find out about the destiny of all those people, and I started working with Ivan Chukhin, whose assistant I was, on the *Karelia Memorial Book*, a compilation of information on 15,000 victims of the Terror. For several years, I went and worked in the archives of the FSB. I wasn't allowed to photocopy anything, so I took in a dictaphone so I could read out the names and write them down at home. For four or five years, I went to bed with a single word on my brain: *"rasstrelyan –* shot". And one day in March 1997, another table appeared in the archives building, for two people researching the Matveyev file and investigating the history of the Solovki convoy. They were Irina Flighe and Veniamin Iofe. We decided to pool our efforts and the following summer, in July 1997, we went to the spot, with my daughter and the dog Koldunya (Witch).'

The Medvezhegorsk local authorities allocated them a group of soldiers to do the digging. Irina, Veniamin, Yury, his daughter, the dog Koldunya and the soldiers made their way to the nineteenth kilometre along the Povenets road, after Pindushi. There is a disused sand quarry there. Elderly people in the area believed they recalled executions taking place there in the past. On the first day, they dug in vain, finding only one bone: from a cow. The next day, Yury set off with a lieutenant and Koldunya to explore the surrounding area. 'While working on the archives, I came across the NKVD's instructions: the site must be far enough away from the road so that anyone passing would not be able to see the fire lit by the escort, or the trucks' headlights, or hear the shots, and also to prevent the prisoners from running away. As I explained all this to the lieutenant, I was scanning the area and I said to myself: "If the Fatherland had given me those orders, where would I have done it?" ' (One hopes, and actually I believe, he wouldn't have done it.) 'Here is too close to the road. A bit further, the fire wouldn't have been visible, but they'd have heard the shots. Further, over there, would be good. At the foot of the third little hill. And while thinking that, I saw all around us square-shaped depressions in the ground, lots of them.' It is important to know (as I learned from Yury and Irina) that the decomposition process of bodies causes the earth to sink by ten to thirty centimetres, and that it is one of the clues that helps pinpoint a former mass grave, as well as a change in the vegetation – grass, for example, or bushes, instead of moss. 'We went back, I brought two soldiers with shovels, and after one and a half hours, I was holding the first skull with a hole in the back of the head.'

5

The place is called Sandarmokh – pronounced 'Sandar-mor' – which means, according to Yury, 'Zachary's marsh' in a mixture of Russian and Karelian. It is at the end of a dirt track, 800 metres to the left of the Povenets road. In winter, access is difficult, the snow sometimes comes up to your waist. 'The ancient forests of the Onega region are majestic and beautiful,' wrote Julius Margolin, a Polish Jew who was deported there in 1940, with tens of thousands of others for having 'illegally crossed the USSR border', as they fled the Nazi advance. 'Winter is the kingdom of white stretches, shimmering opals, a Niagara of snow with amber, azure and rosy dawns like the skies of Italy as depicted in watercolours.' On a rock, at the entrance to the site today, this simple inscription: *Lyudi, ne ubivayte drug druga*, 'People, do not kill one another'. I do not know of any more appropriate inscription than this one, so utterly simple, without any political, religious or historical reference, without inviting revenge or even demanding justice, appealing solely to moral law. There are more than 360 graves of varying sizes in the forest. More than 7,000 people were executed here between 1934 and 1941, including the 1,111 from the Solovki convoy, over five days, on 27 October and then on 1, 2, 3 and 4 November 1937. There are separate memorials to the Polish, Jewish, Muslim, Lithuanian and Ukrainian dead, while beneath the tall red and grey trunks of the pines that filter the light, is another forest, that of the *golubyatni*, the 'dovecotes': a wooden post planted in the ground with a little peaked roof to shelter the dove of the soul. Nailed to the post, a photo of the dead man or sometimes woman, like the beautiful Nina Zakharovna Delibash with a proud gaze, a Georgian economist shot on 1 November 1937 at the age of thirty-four. One of the Solovki convoy, then. It is probably unfair that the beauty of an executed woman should suddenly intensify the emotion you feel when meeting the gaze of the assassinated, but that's the way things are, it has to be acknowledged.

Faces of the forest of the massacred. All speak of life before, probably not great, but bearable, containing a hope of love, family, of promotion, justice, a life that had not yet been destroyed by the state's unfathomable violence. Ivan Alexeyevich Vasilyev, Pavel Nikolayevich Belov, in a soldier's cap. Ivan Yefimovich Maximov, an Orthodox priest in his vestments. Dmitry Trofimovich Kochanov, a shy-looking young man in a tie, his hair slicked back with brilliantine. Alexey Sergeyevich Sergeyev, who bears a resemblance to Faulkner, only pleasanter, more rustic, less arrogant, shot on 1 November 1937. Ivan Ivanovich Mikhaylov, his expression solemn under his cap. Urho Kinnunen, a Finn. Ivan Ivanovich Avtokratov, shot on 2 November 1937. The three Pankratiev brothers, Pavel, Dmitry and Semyon, shot in '37 and '38. Ivan Alexeyevich Yefimov, Alexandr Alexeyevich Vlassov, Andrey Sidorovich Yefimov, Yefim Porfiryevich Dikiye, Anton Yossifovich Nizhinsky, Pyotr Vasilyevich Burakov, with his chubby, smiling face, who worked for the Kondopoga pulp and paper mill and appears (insofar as a snapshot can show these things) to be envisaging a happy future for himself. Matvey Gordeyevich Likhachev, who has a dark moustache, an open, trusting gaze and a shiny shapka. And then Alexey Feodosievich Wangenheim, meteorologist. The artificial flowers make bright splashes of colour among all these dead. The wind rustling the tall pine tree tops, birdsong, no other sound. Infernal scenes once took place in this spot, nowadays so tranquil.

6

The Medvezhegorsk prison. How many there are to a cell, I don't know. His name is called. The guards take him to a hut where his identity is recorded, surname Wangenheim, first name Alexey, patronymic Feodosievich, born on 23 October 1881 in Krapivno, Chernigov province, Soviet Socialist Republic of Ukraine . . . How many times has he answered these questions since the day, nearly four years ago, when Gazov and Chanin locked him up in the Lubyanka . . . He is made to undress, told it is for a medical check-up. He is shoved into another hut, and there, henchmen grab his arms, turn him on to his back, tie his hands and throw him to the floor, put his feet in chains. If he still had any doubts about the fate that awaited him (it is unlikely), at that moment he knows that the Party in which he had put his faith, of which he refused to despair, is going to butcher him like an animal for the slaughter – him and all the others. It is unlikely, and at the same time it is impossible that he could have imagined this abomination.

They remove his wedding ring. Perhaps he tries to struggle, so the killers beat him with truncheons known as *kolotushka* that Matveyev has had made, or with a sort of ice axe which is Bondarenko's preferred instrument. He is dragged into a room where other trussed bodies are already lying, some of them covered in blood. Ingots of human flesh. 'Man is the most precious capital,' wrote Comrade Stalin. When they reach the total, around fifty, the prisoners are tossed on to the two trucks. The booted guards kick them into a heap, spread a tarpaulin over them, sit down on top of it, and the trucks start up. Naked bodies, pressed together, chained, trampled on, bleeding, shivering with cold and fear: that was the unquestionable fraternity born of the Revolution. Is this the kind of thought that goes through their minds? Do people think of anything when they are taken, bound, to the slaughter? It is the beginning of November, the first snow has probably fallen, Lake Onega must be icing over. The trucks crawl forward, bumping over the potholed road, then over the dirt track, headlights jumping in the dark. It takes them nearly an hour to reach their destination. In the forest, a big bonfire is burning, around which the men from the NKVD are keeping warm, smoking, drinking vodka, joking. They are not distressed, they are used to this, they work for the canal camps, and the canal is a great devourer of men. They have dug several graves, not very big, three or four metres by two. There are around twenty of them, and there are other comrades a little further away. Some of them are drunk. There are other graves nearby, freshly covered over, the dug-up earth is still steaming in the cold air. The fire makes giant shadows dance under the trees, sparks whirl up between the trunks. The guards alight from the trucks, ask for help unloading. They must hurry, there's no time to lose, the trucks have to drive back to Medvezhegorsk for another load, they won't be back for two hours. The martyrs are yanked and thrown out of the trucks like logs, they are dragged along the ground, naked or in their underwear, the executioners have padded jackets and shapkas, they jeer at them as well-dressed men can jeer at naked men, as those who are going to live and kill can jeer at those who are going to die, as the Roman centurions jeered at Christ. The dogs bark excitedly. Captain Matveyev finishes his cigarette, throws the butt in the fire, knocks back a slug of vodka, wipes his mouth, jumps into the grave and cocks his Nagant.

7

The only slender satisfaction gained from studying these brutal times is to note that nearly all the killers ended up being shot. Not by popular, international or divine justice, shot not by the Justice, but by the tyranny they served to the point of ignominy. But shot all the same, and it is a relief to know that. You look for their biography, when they have one, and it nearly always ends up with *rasstrelyan*, shot on such-and-such a date. This self-destruction of the executioners reflects the madness of the times. In this case: Yagoda, head of the NKVD, shot, like Prokofyev, his deputy, who had signed Wangenheim's arrest warrant, Yezhov, his successor, shot, Frinovsky, Yezhov's deputy, shot, ditto Apressian and Chanin, two of Wangenheim's interrogators at the Lubyanka, prosecutor Akulov, shot, Major Apeter, head of the Solovki prison camp, shot, Zakovsky and Pozern, two of the Leningrad Special Troika, shot. Not Vyshinsky, unfortunately, he was to have a glorious career as the post-war ambassador to the UN and to die in his own bed, nor

Mikhail Matveyev, the bloodthirsty locksmith. He ended up an alcoholic in Leningrad, thrown out of the NKVD not for the crimes he committed, of course, but because he married an Estonian woman, in other words a potential spy . . .

IV

I have told the story of Alexey Feodosievich Wangenheim, the meteorologist, as scrupulously as possible, without fictionalising, trying to confine myself to what I know. A man who was interested in clouds and did drawings for his daughter, caught up in a history that was an orgy of blood. What was it that suddenly turned his life into a prolonged ordeal of deportation and separation, ending in horror? At what point, on the basis of what slanderous denunciation, what incident that passed unnoticed, what careless joke, was the inevitable process triggered that resulted in his arrest, on 8 January 1934, and then his execution, on 3 November 1937? I don't know exactly, and nor does anybody else, apparently. At that time, it took very little for you to find yourself with the barrel of a revolver pressing against the back of your neck. The most likely – the most plausible – is that the person at the origin of the fatal chain of events was his subordinate Speransky, the person who denounced 'propaganda of foreign origin', 'the blatant Menshevist tendency' in the journal of which Wangenheim was the editor. Perhaps he took the risk of attacking his boss out of cast-iron Lenino-Stalinist conviction, but the most probable explanation is that he did it out of jealousy and ambition. Until 1932, Speransky was at the head of the Hydro-meteorological Department of the Russian Republic, which had been closed down and absorbed into the unified meteorological service of the USSR under Wangenheim. This could have led to bitterness and dreams of revenge. In any case, a denunciation came just at the right time: scapegoats were needed for the catastrophic failure of collectivised farming, and those responsible for the weather forecast were perfect candidates. And in addition to these 'reasons', we shouldn't forget that, under Stalin, all USSR citizens were potentially guilty, it was simply a matter of finding out of what crime, and that was the job of the 'organs'.

I have not glossed over Alexey Feodosievich's faults, when I was aware of them. I have not sought to turn him into an exemplary hero. He was neither a scientific genius nor a great poet, he was in many ways an ordinary man, but he was innocent. Others were quicker to see through Stalin and Stalinism, and realised faster than he did that the 'construction of socialism' was at the price of heavy bloodshed. 'I haven't lost and I never will lose my faith in the Party. There are moments when I lose that trust, but I fight it and will not allow myself to be crushed,' he wrote in June 1934, when he was still in the Kem transit camp; it is not certain that he had grasped just how misplaced his faith was until the very last days, perhaps even the last hours, when already the NKVD henchmen were digging the grave where he would be buried. We cannot know when the light finally dawned; the only thing we can be certain of is that this realisation *in extremis* must have been terrible. Others were more rebellious; I have already mentioned the obdurate Yevgeniya Yaroslavskaya-Markon, who tried to arrange her husband's escape and ended up being shot while shouting abuse at her executioners. Wangenheim was not one of those radical hotheads. He was a man who loved his family, with a very special love for his daughter, his 'little star', a man who loved his profession, and doubtless too the era he lived in, which he believed was a time of great political and scientific conquests. 'May our daughter,' he writes in one of his first letters from the Solovki camp, 'become a worker full of self-sacrifice as we have been. Pass on my passion to her. She will experience times that are even more exciting than ours.' He was a man who perhaps did not question things enough – but it is of course easy to say that three-quarters of a century later. A man, in short, who was worth all of them, and worth the same as anyone, with his honesty and loyalty, and his share of conformism and naivety.

I could claim that it was because he was so 'average' and therefore a sort of Everyman that I embarked on telling the story of his life and death, of his passion: but that would be untrue, to over-sociologise an intention that owes a lot more to happenstance. It was, as I said, the discovery of

Wangenheim's drawings in 2012, at the house of Antonina who has since died; it was the beauty of the place where I made this discovery, that sacred stronghold surrounded by sea (for me, sacred especially because of the human suffering that took place there), it was subsequently meeting people who had known his daughter well, that eventually convinced me to start investigating and then to write. But that is not all, that is not enough. There is something else, something personal which I don't think it is inappropriate to mention now, at the end of this account. What is it that interests me, that concerns me, about this story that is not mine, nor from which I am directly descended? I am not talking about the story of the meteorologist only, but of the terrible era in which he lived and died. And first of all what is it that interests me about this country, Russia, that makes so little effort to be likeable, and which furthermore charms no one – that is an understatement – in the part of the world where I live? No one, myself included, for that matter. And it is not this book that is going to make Russia more likeable . . .

All the same, for nearly thirty years, I have been determined to return. So? Since my first trip in 1986 to the country that was still called the USSR, I must have gone back there more than twenty times . . . so much time stolen from more pleasant destinations . . . At the end of the little book I wrote at the time, *En Russie*, I wondered whether I felt some emotion on leaving a country where I had 'no reason ever to return': although it would seem that I have found plenty of reasons since. The fact is, there is no country in the world that I have visited so assiduously. I had female students in Irkutsk read and commentate on the writings of Henri Michaux and Claude Simon (I fear I wasn't a very good teacher, and that worries me), I stayed in that town where eventually Michael Strogoff, in Jules Verne's 1876 novel, *The Courier of the Czar*, arrived, not without difficulty, longer than in any French town, apart from Paris. I have travelled thousands of kilometres on the Trans-Siberian Railway, four times I visited Vladivostok, I went to the Kamchatka peninsula because it was a name which, in my childhood, meant the end of the world (and that's perhaps the only thing that hasn't changed since my childhood), I went to Khabarovsk to see the river Amur, to Magadan on the Okhotsk Sea because it was the 'moorage of Hades' that Varlam Shalamov writes about, the gateway to the hell of Kolyma. I organised readings by French writers in Moscow, St Petersburg and Yekaterinburg. I tried, with varying degrees of success, to interest numerous audiences, in Omsk, Murmansk and Arkhangelsk-with-its-golden-bells, I went to visit Kant's grave in Kaliningrad, formerly Königsberg, and the cemetery of Eylau, now Bagrationovsk, in memory of Victor Hugo's uncle, Louis-Joseph Hugo, and Balzac's Colonel Chabert. I even spent two weeks in a little village in the Great Siberian North in the company of an excavator of mammoths (an occupation that would have appealed to Eleonora, who became a palaeontologist), and I went from there to the North Pole, or its surrounds. Under the tent of a drifting base, I read *Les Misérables* and talked late into the night (except there was no night), defrosting the vodka in the heat from the kerosene stove, with Russian oceanologists and meteorologists who deployed an array of instruments above and below the ice floe; they had chosen these specialist fields, they told me, in the days of the Soviet Union and the Iron Curtain, because the air and water masses, the winds and the ocean currents knew no frontiers and travelled the world freely. At the time, sadly, I knew nothing of the existence either of Schmidt or of Wangenheim. I would have liked to talk about them with these men.

I am not saying all this to make myself out to be an explorer (others do that very well) or even to flatter myself that I have an in-depth knowledge of Russia. My level of Russian remains pathetic; it has even deteriorated since the days of my early trips. And I have skimmed the surface of this vast country rather than plumbed its depths. I reel off these names, this geography, only to illustrate the curious attraction I mentioned: so many towns crossed, so many horizons gazed at, from the Primorye region, the Far Eastern shore to the Prussian enclave of Kaliningrad, from the rim of the Glacial Ocean to Buryatiya on the border with Mongolia: these areas, and the history that is part of them, or that has been erased, must hold some fascination for me – even if, paradoxically, it is that exerted by some places of horror.

It begins, I believe, with the perception, or rather the feeling, or, on an even more basic level, the giddiness of space. Russia is the high seas on land, I wrote in a short piece, in which I also cite Chekhov ('The power and enchantment of the Taiga is not in its gigantic trees or in its silence, but the fact that only the migrating birds perhaps know where it ends . . .'). A long-distance country. In my Russian tropism there is a geographic element, an attraction to this non-substantial, invisible reality that is space. An elusive power which all the same secretly marks things, of which I have tried to convey a sense, at the beginning of the book, by describing the landscape of infinite plains of Wangenheim's childhood. It is a sensation that we inhabitants of the little European peninsula are not accustomed to, a vast wavelength of the world we are ill-equipped to capture. As Bunin writes in *The Life of Arsenyev*: 'I was born and grew up, as I said, in an absolutely open country such as cannot even be imagined by a European. A vast expanse, with neither obstacles nor boundaries, surrounded me.' And doubtless these expanses exert an even stronger fascination for the heretical European I am because they were prohibited when I was young, and nothing at the time permitted me to foresee that this ban would be lifted during my lifetime. It is that incredulous curiosity that spurred me to go and see what it was like there, in 1986, when the barriers were beginning to come down. The places, things and people I discovered were those to whom the collapse of Communism gave access. The Russian space is inevitably political: history constantly intersects and interweaves with geography. Nothing illustrates this interweaving more than the multiple meanings of the name 'Siberia', at the same time geographical – that continent of plains, hills and marshes where iris bloom, crossed by the Trans-Siberian – and historical, evoking deportation, slavery, camps, suffering, from Dostoevsky's *The House of the Dead*, which opens with the words: 'In the remote parts of Siberia . . .', to Varlam Shalamov's *Kolyma Tales*.

Revolution is the only saga of modern times (in other words of times already gone by) and there are only two universal Revolutions, the French, and in the twentieth century, the Russian. The inhabitants of the twenty-first century will probably forget the worldwide hope created by the October Revolution of 1917, but all the same, for tens of millions of men and women, generation after generation for half a century and on all continents, Communism was the extraordinarily present, vibrant, stirring promise of a dramatic break in the history of humanity, of a new era that was given all sorts of silly names, the glorious future, the rosy future, the infancy of the world, bread and roses – the names were silly but the hope wasn't, and even less the courage placed at the service of this hope – and Soviet Russia seemed to those legions the place where the great upheaval was born, the stronghold of the wretched of the earth. It is amazing to watch the speed at which the huge waves that once shook up the history of the world are obliterated. The memory of that fervent hope is almost lost, but for the generations like mine, for whom 'the Revolution' was still on the horizon, although increasingly blurred, the dream repeated perhaps like a poorly learned lesson rather than revitalised by the fire of experience, it is impossible not to see the former cradle of this universal hope beneath the depressing country it is today, and above all the vast tomb in which it was quickly buried. 'Who will say what the USSR was for us?' wrote Gide, who was certainly not one of the wretched of the earth but one of those among many French intellectuals who were for a while infected by this great enthusiasm. 'More than a chosen land – an example, a beacon. What we have dreamt of, what we have hardly dared to hope, but towards which we were straining all our will and all our strength, was coming into being over there. A land existed where utopia was in process of becoming reality.' Those words were written in 1936, and Gide, recently back from the USSR, was now turning his back on it.

So this 'Russian tropism' is not of course a purely geographical attraction, a sort of aspiration via space, because this space is not solely an expanse, it is not solely abstract or negative, a vanishing line, an absence of confines (although it is that, too): it is peopled by the ghosts of the biggest profane hope there ever was, and of the massacre of that hope, the Revolution and the sinister death of the Revolution. When I speak of Revolution, I am not talking about what it was in reality, of the Bolshevik October coup, the mediocre or paranoid personalities who were its protagonists, the wariness of free thought and the ferocity it displayed from the outset; I am talking of what it was in the dreams of millions, the world changing its basis, the classless society, 'utopia in the process of becoming reality'. An essential part of the history of the twentieth century was played out in this arena, and not only that of the last century, for we still have as a legacy today, even without knowing it, the despair born of that death. That is why this story, in my view, is not talking about a distant planet. The story of the meteorologist, that of all the innocents executed at the bottom of a mass grave, is part of our history insofar as with them a hope was massacred, the hope that we (our parents, those who came before us) shared, a utopia we believed, for a while at least, was in the process of becoming a reality. And the ignominy is so great that it is massacred once and for all. After that, there were plenty of other revolutions, they are national liberation struggles, military putsches, triumphant riots, dramatic turns of events, successful landings, but never again, despite their attempts to seem like a universal message (China, Cuba), would they manage to speak to the entire world, *urbi et orbi*.

It is such a huge ignominy: those hundreds of thousands of dead, in the forests of the night, to quote Blake, in cellars with a gutter or with a sloping floor for the blood to drain away, like water from a shower, or with a tarpaulin that could be hosed down, in quarries, ravines, military camps and trucks, those thousands of skeletons that an excavator unexpectedly digs up beside a motorway or an airport runway, or that are exhumed from a riverbank by floods.

For some of those dead, like the meteorologist, we now know, decades after their assassination, in which grave they lie and can go and place a photo of them with some artificial flowers on the site of their ordeal, but there are still hundreds of thousands of corpses imprisoned in the vast Russian soil, *zemlya*, in places that will perhaps never be discovered. Ultimately, that too is the Russian space: the space of those countless dead.

It is such a huge ignominy: those gazes so hard to sustain, captured on film so that the executioners could be certain they were killing the 'right' person – there were so many condemned that mistakes could be made, the index cards mixed up – that is human – and which are reproduced in the admirable book by the journalist and photographer Tomasz Kizny, *The Great Terror 1937–1938*. The desperate gaze of Alexandra Ivanovna Chubar, executed on 28 August 1938. The fearless expressions of Andrey Vasilyevich Dorodnov, sea rescuer, executed on 20 June 1937, of Semyon Nikolayevich Krechkov, priest, executed on 25 November 1937, the bewildered gaze of Alexandr Ivanovich Dogadov, whose expression, pursed lips, seems to be saying no, this isn't possible, you're going too far, and who would be executed on 26 October 1937, the wide-eyed look of sheer terror of Alexey Grigoryevich Zheltikov, locksmith, executed on 1 November 1937, of Ivan Filippovich Volkov, peat-bog worker, executed on 15 December 1937, the looks of infinite sadness in the eyes of Gavril Sergeyevich Bogdanov, shoveller, executed on 20 August 1937, of Ivan Igorovich Akimov, security guard in a combine, executed on 26 February 1938, the overwhelmed expression of Marfa Ilichna Ryazantseva, her face wrinkled like that of an old apple, executed at the age of seventy-one on 11 October 1937, the incredulous looks of Alexey Ivanovich Zaklyakov, twenty-two-year-old farmhand, executed on 20 August 1937, of Klavdiya Nikolaevna Artemyeva, hairdresser, executed on 29 December 1937, of Ivan Alexeyevich Belokashkin, of no fixed abode, executed on 14 March 1938 at the age of seventeen, of Ivan Mikhaylovich Shalayev, carpenter – his head tilted, his eyes creased, he looks as if he's listening out – the ironic gaze of Germogen Makarevich Orlov, a nineteen-year-old student, executed on 25 January 1938, the defiance in the eyes of Alexandr Kuzmich Lachkov, executed on 10 January 1938, of Boris Yakovlevich Masloboyshchikov, nurse, executed on 21 November 1937, of Gleb Vasilyevich Alexeyev, writer, executed on 1 September 1938, the contemptuous gaze of Mikhail Ivanovich Alatyrtsev, bookkeeper for the Yaroslavl Association of Railway Inventors, executed on 28 May 1938: face raised, half eaten away by shadow, his head swathed in bandages, looking down at the camera, proud, sovereign in misery. And just as the naked bodies heaped in a truck are a concrete image of the fraternity created by the Revolution-become-Terror, those names, those faces of a locksmith, security guard, elderly *babushka*, street child, carpenter, priest, hairdresser, student, nurse, writer, farmhand, make up the countless number of a concrete people, very concretely martyred in the name of the abstraction of a master people.

And the story of all those murdered gazes is our story in yet another way: it is that we have lost interest (our parents, those who came before us). 'The convoys succeeded one another in the forests of the Onega,' wrote Julius Margolin. 'In pleasant France or in South America, proletarian poets composed songs full of emotion about the land of the Soviets.' We are not going to put on trial here those who in our country chose to ignore the vast cemeteries under the Soviet moon, we are not going to remind people of defector Victor Kravchenko or of David Rousset, the French journalist who exposed the Gulag, etc. It is easy to condemn the past, and besides, the story of this blindness is known by those prepared to take the trouble to find out. All the same, this blindness, or indifference, should not be taken lightly. It is not merely incidental. This is how Julius Margolin concludes his *Journey to the Land of the Ze-ka*, one of the great (and magnificently written) testimonies that contribute to the history of the twentieth century: 'A person's behaviour towards the problem of the Soviet camps became the touchstone of my assessment of the individual's honesty. Likewise their behaviour towards anti-Semitism.' Likewise: that is also what author Vasily Grossman – Jewish like Margolin, need we be reminded? – says when he imagines, in *Life and Fate*, a conversation between a Nazi camp commandant and a political commissar prisoner: 'Two poles of one magnet', said the Nazi intellectual to the Soviet intellectual . . . 'Yes, yes, but our victory will be your victory . . . And if you should conquer, then we shall perish only to live in your victory.'

And yet, intellectual philo-Sovietism has had a tough

time, for instance in 1964, when Sartre refused the Nobel Prize for Literature explaining that his 'sympathies undeniably go to socialism and to what is called the Eastern bloc', adding that 'it is regrettable that the Prize was given to Pasternak and not to Sholokhov, and that the only Soviet work thus honoured should be one published abroad and banned in its own country'. (This was twenty years after he had fallen out with Arthur Koestler over *Darkness at Noon*, and the year when Vasily Grossman died in Moscow, alone, rejected, excluded from all the intellectual circles, dispossessed of his great book, the manuscript of which was 'arrested' by the KGB.) An appalling statement, because it appears to be saying (it does say) that it is to Pasternak's discredit that he is banned in the USSR. But let us move on. (Sartre was heard and Sholokhov received the Nobel Prize the following year.) More interesting perhaps than settling scores with ghosts is the following consideration: in the West people tend to be largely ignorant of the horrendous history of 'real socialism', and consequently a huge chunk of the century we come from, which we refer to as 'terrible', has been lost. Half of the terror of that terrible century, half of the darkness of that nocturnal century. In *Journey to the Land of the Ze-Ka* there is a conversation between a Soviet engineer and the prisoner Margolin. 'Today,' says Margolin, I know exactly how I feel about the Soviet Union: and that is fear. Before arriving in this country, I had never been afraid of men. But the USSR has taught me to be afraid of man.' Words that echo others, by Nadezhda Mandelstam wife of the poet

Osip Mandelstam: 'Of all the things we have experienced, the most fundamental and the strongest is fear . . . fear has destroyed everything that ordinarily makes up a human life.' We have barely concerned ourselves with that immense fear, variously reflected, suffered, confronted, overcome, in hundreds of thousands of gazes. Today we are justifiably alarmed at seeing the risk of the inhuman resurface in Russia, but our alarm would be more credible if we had paid attention to what was human in the history of this country, and that humanity was first and foremost that of the victims.

EPILOGUE

EPILOGUE

I might have met Eleonora, the meteorologist's daughter, the recipient of the drawings and plant collections. I missed her by a year. She became a palaeontologist, an expert on vertebrates. She worked at the Laboratory of Quaternary Stratigraphy of the Institute of Geology of the Russian Academy of Sciences. She did not marry, never celebrated her birthday, forbade anyone from mentioning that date. She was an accomplished pianist, smoked two packets of cigarettes a day (no connection between these two facts). Each year she attended the remembrance ceremony at Sandarmokh.

On 28 December 2011, there was a little New Year's Eve party at the lab. Eleonora was there and asked to be allowed to work during the coming holiday. On 4 January, she telephoned a colleague to wish her son a happy birthday. That day and the following days, 5, 6, 7 and 8 January, she went to the lab, where she worked alone. On the 7th, she promised to pay a visit to Memorial's office the following week. The 8th was the anniversary of her father's arrest. I do not draw any conclusions, but I have to point it out, as it was pointed out to me. On the 9th, the last day of the new year holiday, at 1.24 p.m., she called one of her colleagues from her mobile phone and asked if she would be at work the next day. 'In case I don't come in,' Eleonora said, 'I've left you a little package.' Less than an hour after that call, her body was found at the foot of the apartment building where she lived on the ninth floor, at 12 Michurinsky Prospekt.

The following day, at the lab, her colleagues found all her instructions for her cremation and the place where the urn should be deposited. She strictly forbade them to organise a funeral meal. During the holiday, she had tidied her office and set aside the books to be returned to the library. Thus ends, seventy-four years after his death, the story of the meteorologist.

Acknowledgements

I could not have written this book without the assistance of Irina Flighe and Yury Dmitriev from the Memorial association: I thank them, and also my friend Valery Kislov, who helped me translate the many documents from the NKVD archives, and Vasily Potapov, himself a meteorologist, who gathered them and copied them out by hand.

I also thank Svetlana Dolgova and Emmanuel Durand, of publishers Paulsen Co. Ltd, Russia, and lastly Varvara Voyetskova, for maintaining her good humour during the long days of work in Moscow.

Even if I have been careful to be as precise and exact as possible, this book is not a scholarly work. So I have not systematically cited the historians whose work I referred to, but of course, for everything relating to the general background of the Great Terror, I am indebted to the works of Anne Applebaum, Robert Conquest, and especially (with regard to the NKVD Operational Order 00447) of Nicolas Werth.

penguin.co.uk/vintage